CUTTING EDGE

CUTTING EDGE

John Smith
with Elizabeth Gibson

MONARCH
TUNBRIDGE WELLS

Copyright © John Smith and Elizabeth Gibson 1992
The right of John Smith to be identified
as author of this work has been asserted by him in
accordance with the Copyright, Design
and Patents Act 1988.

First published 1992

Published in collaboration with the
Greenbelt Christian Arts Festival

ISBN 1 85424 165 6

Unless otherwise indicated, biblical quotations are from the
New International Version © 1973, 1978, 1984 by the
International Bible Society.

British Library Cataloguing in Publication Data
A catalogue record for this book is available from
the British Library.

Production and Printing in England for
MONARCH PUBLICATIONS
Owl Lodge, Langton Road, Speldhurst, Kent TN3 0NP
by Nuprint Ltd, Harpenden, Herts AL5 4SE

Dedication

Dedicated to Dr Athol Gill—Servant-scholar, trouble-maker for God, champion of the poor, companion along the Way, mentor, dreamer and friend—in the hope that the questions he raised, both profound and obvious, will find passionate and committed responses from those of us he befriended and discipled.

Contents

INTRODUCTION:
Two Sacred Cows to Set Aside

Many people are on the edge economically, emotionally, socially, sexually, politically and spiritually—in every way. But what about those of us who call ourselves Christians?

Most of us like to think that we have found the answers to life's questions: that once we are walking with God our lives will run smoothly. We don't like to think of ourselves as in any way on the edge: we use words like 'saved'—as if, somehow, in knowing Jesus, we are now pulled back from the brink. But are we?

Much to the dismay of the pious people of his time, Jesus began life on the edge, he continued it there, and he ended it there. Born in a cave or cattlestall at the back of an obscure home in Bethlehem, in the backwater of a tiny, powerless country called Judea, he owned nothing beyond his tools for carpentry. His life was in constant danger: hounded by lawyers, scribes, and Pharisees, and bound up with a motley crew of dissident fishermen, zealots, tax collectors and prostitutes. When he died it was in the absolute humiliation of nakedness on the crossed timbers of foreign overlords, stripped and nailed down for daring to speak (and be) the truth.

How then can we call ourselves Christians and not expect to be on the edge? Jesus is still on the edge. His

Spirit lives with those on the rubbish dumps of Manila and Mexico City: with the unwanted and dying babies tossed out into Calcutta gutters; with those staring at death because their drinking has finally precipitated cirrhosis of the liver; with refugees fleeing war and famine; with abused children and lonely widows; with HIV carriers; with single mothers waiting in a queue for unemployment and family benefits that don't begin to meet their financial needs; with those imprisoned, tortured and exploited. He is with them all—with us all. And when we pray that radical prayer Jesus taught us, 'Your kingdom come, your will be done', we are committing ourselves to living on the edge with Jesus and with the poor, despised, hurting and dispossessed of the earth.

Either/or theology

For generations Christians have argued whether the most important aspect of faith and the best reflection of the kingdom of God on earth is the presence of God and his people, or the proclamation of the good news. *Presence and proclamation.* Some so-called 'liberals' have championed the former, getting their hands dirty with work among the suffering victims of greed, disease, and broken relationships; often looking actually embarrassed about the evangelistic fervour of some of their Christian brothers and sisters. So-called 'evangelicals' (and these labels rarely help anyone) have meanwhile majored on preaching and building up Christian fellowship, often responding in reactionary and critical ways to the rabid activism of their 'liberal' counterparts: Anything to avoid living on the edge with the wounded, or being one of the wounded themselves. It's so much easier, isn't it, to escape the painful tension by falling down on one side or the other!

Have we heard the words of Jesus that his kingdom is in our midst? I often wonder if we have! They are threatening words, for they do not hold out offers of a cosy, comfortable life without pain. We want heaven, all right, but we talk about it as being 'up there': always it's somewhere where we aren't, because we're 'down here'. But Jesus has made a nonsense of such thinking, and the mediaeval cosmology of up/down needs to go the way of the claim that the earth is flat, and that it's at the centre of the universe! The Incarnation once and for all gives the lie to up/down theology; Jesus has become flesh and dwelt among us. He is Emmanuel—God with us. We can sentimentalise his life and ring it round with glittering gold stars and haloes, but there was of course nothing pretty about the birth at Bethlehem nor the crucifixion at Calvary.

This determination to see the kingdom in an either/or, black/white, up/down way has wasted a woeful amount of energy in the church. Until we have the courage to live in the painful tension between the two extremes, seeing that the gospel includes both proclamation and presence, then we are frantically pulling away from the Jesus of Bethlehem and the Jesus of the gospels. Until we face the pain of our own and others' marginalisation, we are numbing ourselves with analgesics, wrapping ourselves in protective plastic. And in so doing we are losing touch with the heart of God.

This is a frightening thought, one we shrink away from. But many times Jesus told us, 'Follow me.' He wasn't only promising in these words to lead us into a happier, safer, sweeter life; he was promising that he would lead us, and ask us to help lead others, into a just kingdom. Life isn't about religious bits and non-religious bits. It's a seamless whole. The only material legacy Jesus left behind was a seamless coat, over which his murderers argued and finally settled the debate by gambling for it. We can't separate sacred and secular because Jesus doesn't. We can't separate proclamation and presence because Jesus doesn't. When he announced his divine call and mandate after painful contemplation and temptation in the Judean desert, he pronounced captives free and declared his anointing to proclaim the gospel to the poor (Luke 4:18–19). Likewise, when John the Baptiser lost his nerve in prison, requiring evidence that Jesus *was* the just one of whom he had preached, Jesus sent the assurance that the Kingdom was one of words *and* works (Luke 7:18–23). 'Go and tell John what you have SEEN AND HEARD,' he said.

For Christians there can be no either/or theology. We've got to face up to the challenge of both/and, not only/but also theology. It's not just a case of proclaiming the need for forgiveness, repentance and faith; it's also a case of living out Christ's presence, as his body here on this broken earth, in full repentance: repentance which means not only are we radically transformed within, but also that we help God in the creative work of remaking the world. 'Your kingdom come, your will be done on earth as it is in heaven.' There is no way to live the both/and theology except on the edge.

Room with a Western view

It's a peculiarly Western worldview that makes us try to separate secular and sacred, social and spiritual. When we apply this false thinking we are shortchanging the gospel and we're missing out on an understanding of God himself. We may feel safer when we compartmentalise the world in this way and we may feel further from the frightening edge, but we'll also be choosing to place ourselves further from God.

God is about relationships. Logic and love are married in Christ. In his very Person, God is relational: Father, Son and Spirit. When he calls us to him, and when we hear His call, we are awakening to the realisation that we are his children. In turn that makes us brother and sister to the rest of God's people: those who know him, and those who do not. In turn that makes us brother and sister to all creation. Individualism simply won't lead us into gospel truth. If we pray 'Your kingdom come,' we're praying for improved relationships in *all* God's creation.

In the West we are so steeped in the idea that we must take control of our own lives that we can't seem to see how insidious and all-pervasive our individualism is. The West values enterprise, achievement, image, and careful, neatly structured organisations with as few loose ends as possible. Accordingly many decisions—political, social, economic—are made on the basis of the survival of the fittest and the fitting of the survivors, not on the basis of compassion.

We work hard and therefore think we have a right to be privileged and have power; but the gospel is about pain. We project successful images and turn our eyes away from the open sores of truth; but the gospel is about prophecy and clear-sightedness. We hoard possessions with unthinking greed, shoring ourselves up against feared 'disasters' with rampant consumerism; but the gospel is about sharing, caring, and compassion for those who truly live in disaster. We silence the cries of anguish from without and within with charismatic choruses or strident rock music; but the gospel is about peace, provision, and mercy. We worship sex, music, and even the church; but the gospel is about worshipping the Living God who alone can fill the aching void. We claim to love peace and somehow overlook the violence that turns dreams to nightmares all around us; but the gospel is about healing and forgiveness.

The kingdom in our midst

Once and for all our cherished sacred cows of either/or theology and Western individualism need to be put out to pasture. The gospel isn't about taking control. It's about letting go, surrendering the self to live and even fall off the edge—and into the loving kingdom of God.

It's my prayer, then, that as you read this book you will not only experience the blessed presence of Jesus in your life, but also that you will come to share his both/and agenda, growing in wisdom about what is really happening in our broken world, and what we can do, together, about it.

John Smith

1

Called to Privilege and Power...
or Pain?

> They went to a place called Gethsemane, and Jesus said to
> his disciples, 'Sit here while I pray.' He took Peter, James
> and John along with him, and he began to be deeply
> distressed and troubled. 'My soul is overwhelmed with
> sorrow to the point of death,' he said to them. 'Stay here
> and keep watch.'
>
> Going a little farther he fell to the ground and prayed
> that if possible the hour might pass from him. 'Abba,
> Father,' he said, 'everything is possible for you. Take this
> cup from me. Yet not what I will, but what you will.'
>
> Then he returned to his disciples and found them sleep-
> ing. 'Simon,' he said to Peter, 'are you asleep? Could you
> not keep watch for one hour? Watch and pray so that you
> will not fall into temptation. The spirit is willing, but the
> body is weak.'
>
> (Mark 14:32–38)

In the olive grove of Gethsemane Jesus looked pain in
the face. He was just as frightened as we would be. He
knew he needed friends with him, but he understood
equally how vulnerable and weak even loving friends can
be.

We may read that story and wonder what it has to do
with us. Separated by two thousand years and by two
quite different cultures—Western from Eastern—we're
tempted to think much more of Jesus' promises that our

burdens will be easy and light if we follow him, than about standing with him in places of pain. Yet that is exactly what he asked his friends to do in Gethsemane. And it is exactly what he asks us to do in today's Gethsemanes if we call ourselves his friends and followers.

One of my long-time favourite songs is 'Summertime' from George Gershwin's blues opera *Porgy and Bess*. Few songs make me cry more easily because it's a song which has such depth and sensitivity. A black mother is bringing her child into the cottonfields, into the midst of human slavery and suffering. She is full of hopes and dreams. Her joys are the simple pleasures of the poor which the rich rarely feel in ordinary observations like jumping fish and growing cotton. She knows that the world is not as she would like it to be, but she also knows, instinctively, that it should be as in her dreams.

> Summertime and the living is easy
> Fish are jumpin'
> And the cotton is high
> Oh your daddy is rich
> And your ma is good lookin'
> So hush little baby—don't you cry
>
> One of these mornings
> You're gonna rise up singin'
> You'll spread your wings
> And you'll take to the skies

If you are a person who dreams, I am writing for you. Young people (especially) are full of dreams. The sadness is that these dreams are soon numbed by the drugs of this artificial world; we anaesthetise ourselves against pain and true pleasure by consumerism, television, magazines, music, and all the other trappings of Western individualism and selfishness. We distance ourselves from suffering and arrange our lives to fit in with the rest of this 'analgesic' society. We run away from conflict and say we can't cope. To make matters even less painful for ourselves, we hide our knowledge of the pain by using euphemistic language ('friendly fire' to refer to the tragic shooting of nine UK soldiers by other Allied troops in the Gulf War, for instance). Then we move into our own cosy little comfort zones, shut the door, and carry on as if none of the pain had anything to do with us.

Can Christians afford to live this way? I don't think so. When God calls us—often as young people—to dream dreams of a different world, he doesn't call us into the comfort zone, much as we wish he did. Instead, he asks us to identify with people who are suffering, with the poor of the world rather than the rich. In this respect we simply can't ignore the way he went about his own ministry. Did he preach the good news about going to heaven? No. He preached about his special kingdom: a different way, a different law, different values, a different life, a different hope and perspective. He didn't say, 'Seek first a high standard of comfort, and the kingdom shall be given to you', but 'Seek first his kingdom and his righteousness (justice), and all these things will be given to you as well' (Matthew 6:33). And as he preached, he healed people in all kinds of suffering.

There wasn't a crippled leper, a hungry child, an exhausted woman—or even a black woman singing a lullaby to her child—whose pain escaped his eyes. His heart went out to them all: 'Filled with compassion, Jesus reached out his hand and touched the man... "Be clean!" Immediately the leprosy left him and he was cured' (Mark 1:41–42); 'When Jesus landed and saw a large crowd, he had compassion on them, because they were like sheep without a shepherd' (Mark 6:34). In his ministry, he showed that it wasn't enough to mouth platitudes about love; instead he taught us to live that compassion. (The words used in the New Testament Greek to describe Jesus' response to human suffering actually suggest that his guts were knotted with anguish for those in pain; he knew—and knows now—that to ease suffering, we have to share it.) 'Surely he has borne *our* griefs and carried our sorrows' (Isaiah 53:3, 4, RSV).

Ideally, the Christian community should be the most thoughtful, the most creative, the most committed. As St Iranaeus, one of the early church fathers, put it, 'The glory of God is a human being fully alive.' Somehow, I don't think that means life in the comfort zone. No one can tell me that Jesus would have looked on 'orthodox' evangelical theology as more important than the suffering of human beings on the receiving end of corrupt and hypocritical systems. We need, then, to move out of our intellectual, social, and religious huddles and identify with the poor, marginalised and alienated: hearing what they have to say, and listening both to God and to the world—with the ears and eyes of the poor.

It's not that our own day-to-day upheavals and sorrows aren't of concern to God, but that we need to see them, as he does, in the perspective of real tragedies in the rest of the world—the two-thirds world which we'd rather shut out. We can no longer claim to have sole franchise on the gospel when Jesus died as much for the two-thirds world as for us. Do we want to gloat over the now commercialised glories of the Grand Canyon, or do we want to sit down on the rim of it and listen to the stories of the native American Indians who have lost their land to Western greed? Do we want to turn up the volume of our charismatic praise and worship, or do we want to respond to the laments of the downtrodden who call to us from street corners and cardboard boxes in Waterloo? These are painful questions with distinctly uncomfortable answers.

It is worth noting that at the very time the UN is admitting the abject failure of 40 years' attack on world poverty, and projecting a massive increase of poverty into the 21st century, the collapse of the Eastern bloc invites the West to self-interested isolationism. The US, which once cried to the world 'send us your poor'—now relieved of the need to court the third world in a political cold war scenario—is retreating from global responsibility and from its own poor. The greatest obscenity of all is that the one nation which can lay claim to the most Christian foundations may now lead the world in withdrawal from global issues of justice and care.

Places of pain

The destitute, those who have been deserted, the needy, the lonely, the uneducated, those who do not know their rights, the dispossessed—who are they? In many countries, pregnant teenagers account for many such people in pain. In Australia—my country—bikers and Aborigines would have to be included in the list. In parts of Continental Europe and the British Isles, gypsies are the marginalised ones. In the Middle and Near East it is the refugees of the Gulf War, the homeless and poison gassed, the Kurds, the Afghans—all who have been driven out by struggles over religion and land in those volatile countries. In China it's those who dare to seek personal and political freedom. And in South Africa it's the dispossessed of the black townships. Pain is all around and within us, and we ignore it at our peril. God longs for us to stand up boldly and declare, 'I want to heal with Jesus, feel with Jesus, see with Jesus. I'm going to get moving with the legs of Jesus, empowered by the muscles of faith he's already given me. I'm going to stand with him in Gethsemane.'

If we dare to take that stand, we are moving away from the idea that 'I love you' means 'I need you'; away from the neurosis that is borne of greed ('I've got so many things, whom can I trust, and how can I have time to do anything for anyone else?'); away from loneliness, introversion, and broken relationships which come from greed and lack of sensitivity to the world God's given us. So let's set aside our analgesics—the comfortable things we use to numb us to the pain around us—and see a little of that world of pain. No one who is old enough to feel physical and emotional pain is unable to face the tough questions raised at the point where politics and pain intersect.

In 1988 I made a visit to El Salvador that I'll certainly never forget. We had made our way into one particular valley, an isolated area normally only accessible by helicopter, by climbing down the mountainside, intending to bring aid to the war refugees there from some Christians in the US. We received a terrific greeting from them; they were overjoyed to meet Westerners who genuinely seemed to care, but I felt humbled—anything but heroic—as they told us of the events of the previous day.

An American military helicopter had flown in and out again just before we arrived. The El Salvadorean air force uses US helicopters—just a small part of the millions of dollars of military aid per year for one of the world's most brutal regimes. The carriers had swooped on what little food was left to refugees already reduced to living under shelters constructed of plastic bags and pieces of wood. They snatched up the sparse piles of maize accumulated by women whose husbands had been murdered or 'disappeared'—and took almost all of it. Before they left, they asked for the leader and Bible teacher of the community as well, and took him. The last we heard he had never been seen again.

When I saw what was left, I wanted to weep. Maize grown on those steep mountainsides is marginal anyway, with so little rain to penetrate the thin soil. Often only one kernel in five forms properly; it's not even fit to feed cattle and pigs. Still, the refugees themselves were not at all self-pitying. They sat singing and offering us tortillas made of the last of the maize; they would rather have died from lack of food than have lost their sense of communion—of sharing, compassion, and commitment—their sense of thankfulness to us. In their faces I saw reflected a gentle reproach to all the emptiness and shallowness of the Western Christian church; I was ashamed and moved.

Eastern Europe

I have a chunk of the Berlin Wall on my desk at home, courtesy of my daughter Kathy, and it means a lot to me. Then aged 18, she found herself in Berlin during the week when the Wall finally came down. Somehow she got a small pickaxe and laid into a section of the Wall. She sent us home that piece of wall with a photograph to prove that she hadn't bought it from an opportunist. It's a most unimpressive bit of Socialist concrete, but it reminds me to thank God for the end of the tyranny of at least one power-hungry group of people over another.

It also reminds me that tyranny takes many forms, some less easy to spot than others. As everyone now knows, it wasn't long after the Wall came down that the speculators and property developers (supposedly motivated by the noble ideals of Western enterprise and democracy) moved in to exert their own brand of tyranny in East Germany. Hardly had the first chunks of masonry hit the ground when the scramble began—developers buying land from the East side, then jacking up the prices so that the average East Berliner could never hope to afford it later. It's frightening to think, too, that many of those speculators were self-professed Spirit-filled Christians.

If the jostling for land in the new world post glasnost is scary, what about the jostling for flesh? The BBC reported recently about a Russian gynaecologist who decided to turn his experience of women to a more lucrative use after perestroika had eased the controls on sexual practices in his country. He closed up his surgery and opened a sleazy training centre for young women who wanted to boost their earnings and 'improve' their lifestyles by becoming striptease performers. Counting on the anxiety and vulnerability of students and other marginalised young women, he promised them a new life in the West once they were fully trained. We can only guess at the pain these women are facing now.

The Philippines

In 1989 my wife, Glena, and I went with members of our church in Melbourne to the Philippines. We were preparing for the Lausanne Congress on World Evangelization. Because of the way our flights were arranged, we actually arrived three days before our official responsibilities were due to begin. Rather than idling the time away, we decided to make contact with some of the human rights workers we knew there and to offer our services.

We knew what we were getting into. People in Europe may not know much about the Philippines beyond a few stories of Ferdinand and Imelda Marcos (of shoe-fetish fame), or of Cory Aquino, widow of the murdered radical who had challenged the Marcos dictatorship. But Glena and I knew all too well of the assassinations and death squads which characterise life and death in these islands, and how the houses of 'questionable' people are raked with government or vigilante bullets.

Only a few months before, two members of our staff, whilst visiting Mindanao, had been fired on by a government soldier as they were working on a human rights investigation. Just eight weeks previously a number of people had been executed by the military because of their uncompromising stand on human rights—a stand taken bravely against the corrupt and violent system of the Philippines generally. The army had told a garbled tale about the deaths of those protesters, and my colleagues were helping other human rights investigators to dig up the bodies in an effort to discover the truth from ballistic evidence. They escaped the gunfire, but only narrowly. It's likely that if my colleagues hadn't been there (concerned Westerners are especially valuable because they may provide a sort of cover against human rights abuses), the Filipinos leading the investigation would have been unhesitatingly wiped out.

Since Cory Aquino's rise to power, a few of the more flagrant injustices and abuses of the Marcos regime have been removed. But sadly, Westerners have turned away from the situation and assumed things have now become more comfortable for the poor. Of course this is not the case. Even someone who is receiving the backing of the army and other authorities cannot clean up chaos overnight in a place like the Philippines—as Mrs Aquino has discovered.

After her first starry-eyed six months, the honeymoon was over. The army grew restless. Poverty still reigned, people were hungry, death squads roamed the streets looking for human rights lawyers and activists.

Speculators came after peasants' land, and power and patronage drove what was left of the shredded economy. As Nobel Prize nominee Bishop Fortich expressed it to my wife, 'We were once ruled by Ali Baba and the forty thieves. Now Ali Baba is dead but the forty thieves continue to rule.' We had a taste of that chaos ourselves that year. One of our church members was picked up on his way to the WCE conference by local police. They drove him out of town, robbed him of everything he had and threw him out of the car. A small taste of other much worse happenings (the army had robbed a major bank in the capital, Manila, not long before), perhaps, but a salutary lesson in corruption for all of us. Of course one must ask the question—How can a country, ruled for a century, economically, militarily and politically by the interests of the most Christian democracy on earth, be the fifth poorest nation on earth?

Our Filipino friends took us up on our offer of help. Glena was asked to go to the island of Negros to help the aforementioned Catholic priest, Bishop Fortich. He was struggling to protect 700 internal refugees who were on the point of assassination by vigilantes after their displacement by military operation—Operation Thunderbolt. The Filipino government had been scouring the mountains for a handful of the rebel New People's Army (NPA). In search of the NPA, they drove 30,000 people from their homes and farms, destroyed their crops, provided no food, medicine or accommodation and accused them of sheltering the NPA. 'You're all sympathisers,' these peasant farmers had been told, 'we'll shoot the lot of you.'

Glena went gladly to be one of three Western observers to make sure there were no more government or vigilante atrocities on these dispossessed people. Of the original 30,000, many died of disease and ambush by vigilantes. About 1,000 found their way to the seminary where Bishop Fortich offered to disrupt seminary programmes to shelter and provide for them. On the way, two or three hundred refugees had already been killed and the priest was determined that no more should be caught by sniper fire or decapitated by vigilantes.

At the seminary Glena met the Bishop working out of an office that was peppered with bullet holes and scarred by a hand grenade which had almost cost him a leg. A group of eighty seminarians provided him with his only support. Working with almost no facilities, the men laboured to house, clothe, doctor and feed the refugees. 'The seminarians are certainly learning what the Christian faith is all about,' the priest told Glena.

The vigilantes had followed the refugees right to the edge of the seminary grounds. When the priest organised a basketball game between the refugees, seminarians and local villagers, several refugees spotted the same vigilantes who had murdered their families and driven them from the mountains. Panic spread like wildfire. Realising that they had been recognised, the vigilantes commandeered the local radio station and announced that unless the refugees returned to the mountains (where they would have been slaughtered by the army as NPA sympathisers), they would be massacred by the selfsame vigilantes. Glena was one of the three from the WCE conference, there to embarrass the vigilantes, who would thus be under Western eyes on the day of the promised slaughter. Her courage and the courage of those who went with her contributed to the establishment of what was to become a permanent monitoring group at the seminary to protect the refugees.

While Glena was in Negros, I went to a town on the island of Mindanao. I knew what was going on in Negros and asked for the WCE daily prayer bulletin at the conference to include prayer for the 700 refugees at the seminary. To my dismay, I was refused—not just for the expected reasons of red tape at such short notice, but because the story of the refugees was considered 'too hot' politically. Frantic attempts to raise sympathy from conference organisers and the distribution of several hundred copies of Bishop Fortich's telegrammed request for conference delegates to come, aroused mostly embarrassed dismissal or muted sympathy. The Moderator of the Uniting Church of Australia, Victorian Synod, Reverend David Uren and the Director for Evangelism in the NY diocese of the Episcopal Methodist Church USA, were the lone companions of my wife in her courageous response to the Bishop's urgent plea. Several major figures, including the Archbishop of the Anglican Church in Victoria, Australia, expressed their wish to join the group, but were unable to do so because they had to address the plenary sessions of the conference.

On Mindanao the mayor of one town had gone slightly mad. The town has a history of mutilations, rapes, beheadings and other atrocities for anyone who speaks up for human rights, and the mayor seemed thirsty for yet more pain and bloodshed. Pretending to launch a civic building programme on some land belonging to the federal government, he ruthlessly bulldozed all the houses of the poor. I should mention that these were not shanty or slum dwellings, but substantial homes constructed from concrete blocks and timber. When the people fled to the town hall, he bulldozed that too, leaving the villagers homeless and crying for Western observers to come in and photograph what had happened. His private reasons apparently concerned gold allegedly buried on the land by the Japanese during their World War II invasion.

I flew out with a number of other Christians and human rights activists, including my Australian co-pastor, Martyn, one lawyer whose brother had been murdered the week before, and a young woman whose parents' home had been destroyed that very day, while her brother had also been assassinated the week before.

The townspeople greeted us rapturously, especially when they saw the lawyer, whom they knew as their friend and advocate. This pint-sized lady was one with whom the village women particularly identified. The bulldozing was still in full swing, women and children tugging on our clothes, weeping, crying hysterically as the bulldozers rumbled towards their homes. It was the heroic lawyer who braved the bulldozers and cried 'Come on!' as we went in with our cameras.

The military men and demolition crews fell back in surprise and alarm. As we wielded our cameras, soldiers ran off in fright and uncertainty, so we grew bolder. Martyn and I climbed onto an abandoned bulldozer and tried to rip out the wires to incapacitate it. When that failed, we took to kicking at the power box. Then came a moment I'll never forget, a moment when prophecy, pain and the possibility of death all came together for me...a vigilante holding a deadly M16 assault rifle stopped right by the bulldozer and levelled the rifle at us, warning us sharply in English that he was going to shoot.

Strangely, it wasn't the gun that drew my eyes, but the T-shirt he was wearing. It proclaimed Jesus. Something snapped inside me, and I don't think I could ever have preached again if I hadn't spoken up. Poking my finger at his chest, I shouted, 'How dare you wear Jesus' name on your T-shirt? The Jesus of the Bible is the God of the widow and the fatherless. How can you oppress these women and children and destroy their homes?'

I stared into the throat of the rifle and prayed some quick prayers for Glena and the children. The soldier hesitated. Then a more senior officer ran up behind him waving a repeater handgun and screaming obscenities at Martyn and me for stopping the bulldozing. Martyn continued photographing the approaching officer. The bulldozing was over, for that day at least, and we were carted off to prison for what was a very frightening night.

The pain of the people of that town goes on. Are we going to sit comfortably while the poor grow poorer? Or can we identity with them by writing letters to Amnesty International and to our own governments, demanding that the myth of improved human rights in the Philippines (and elsewhere) be replaced with reality and commitment? As Jesus stood in Gethsemane and prayed 'Not my will but Thine' (not my deliverance but theirs), the decision to stand up for justice and love was one we could not avoid. Repeated pleas for our release from two UN representatives, and a noble Filipino Congressman, fell on deaf ears. The mayor declared his intention to execute, not only us, but also the officers who failed to kill us on the spot. Only the international release of our plight through Reuters by courageous human rights journalists who visited us, saved the day.

No one reading this chapter can feel comfortable, and I

don't feel comfortable writing about the pain either. It's completely human to be terrified of pain—just as Jesus and his disciples were on the night before the Crucifixion. If we were truly to look the world's pain in the face, as Jesus did that night and again the next day, we would find it hard to function any more. So, instead, we trivialise it by sandwiching it between inane advertisements and game shows: or we blot it out by escaping into our careers, our status symbols or analgesics like drugs, alcohol, music, or sex. As Westerners—especially white middle-class males—we no longer know how to weep.

The wonderful news is that God understands our fear and failure. As our heavenly parent he understands our weakness. 'He tends his flock like a shepherd. He gathers the lambs in his arms and carries them close to his heart; he gently leads those that have young' (Isaiah 40:11). He offers comfort even to the most downcast—look at the Books of Psalms and Lamentations if you're feeling 'out of it' while some of your Christian friends smile and clap and sing! As a 'man of sorrows and acquainted with grief', he knows that we will resist him but that in the end the only way we can follow him is along the paths of pain that he also trod. 'By this, all will know that you are my disciples, if you love one another' (John 13:35). Jesus carries still the scars of his Crucifixion, and we, made in his image, can't expect to go through life unscarred. A Christian is some-one who, above all else, opts to follow and live like Jesus— through the Spirit's power, and through a conscious decision. And there is no way to live like Jesus without pain and contradiction.

There's a lie abroad that the best way for a Christian to grow spiritually is to be isolated from failure and suffering. It's just that—a lie. The great ones of the Bible were those who, rather than getting swallowed up in their own selfish concerns, spoke for God even as they stood in places of pain. So it's definitely worth thinking more about pain to discover what a gift it in fact is to the human race—not at all the destructive enemy we call it. I would even dare claim that it is the greatest single gift we can have. It offers over-fed, over-counselled, and over-amused Westerners an opportunity to step outside their own (often self-induced) psychological alienation and taste the human realities of suffering in the two-thirds world. It teaches us compassion—a word that means 'suffering with' others. It teaches us vulnerability, too, without which there is no room for God to work in our lives. 'How else can the Lord Christ enter in,' someone once wrote, 'but through a broken heart?' A Latin proverb declares 'Shattered glass reflects the most light.'

A few years ago I managed to severely prolapse two discs in my back. After months of crippling pain and deterioration, facing a journey to America and Britain, I sought advice from an osteopath and also an orthopaedic surgeon for a diagnosis, and the news wasn't good. The discs were bulging out between the two adjoining vertebrae and threatening to split. The surgeon's prognosis included the necessity for spinal fusion but the likelihood of success was small. He gave me some anti-inflammatory pills and added 'Smith, do nothing. Lie down and read or listen to music.' The pills eased the pain, dulled the mind, but did nothing to change the condition. Pills and thrills are a mark of our analgesic society—it feels better but it gets worse. The osteopath knew I wouldn't listen—and that I would pay for it in pain. The pain, including severe sciatic nerve responses, was there to warn me of worse damage to come if I ignored it. (An extraordinary experience in Jerusalem in the Garden of Gethsemane was to totally heal the condition some weeks later.)

Whether emotional or physical, pain warns us when we are behaving like idiots. If, then, we want to know the joy of a full Christian life; if we want to discover the full joy of our humanity—we ought not to evade pain. We cannot legitimately claim the title 'Christian' and live a life of avoiding and escaping pain. Rather, we have to embrace our pain—and others' pain—until its intensity drives us to act. And if we feel no pain at the state of the world, maybe it's time we went out into those places of pain and human suffering I've described and took on ourselves the sharing of others' pain.

We need to look for the causes of pain. Are they greed or selfishness rather than poverty and broken relationships? When we know the true causes, we then have to ask for God's help in forgiving and curing the pain.

In the interim pain leads us into truth, it clarifies our commitments, and it provokes questions.

Pain and reality

Failure and suffering bring us eyeball to eyeball with reality. It's not when we're successful and comfortable that we deal in reality, for at those times we're more likely to be enmeshed in the fantasies and lies we spin out of commerce and entertainment. Rather, it's when everything in our world seems to have caved in that we are most blessed, most in touch with God and his truth:

> Blessed are the poor in spirit,
>   for theirs is the kingdom of heaven.
> Blessed are those who mourn,
>   for they shall be comforted....
> Blessed are those who are persecuted because of righteousness,
>   for theirs is the kingdom of heaven.
>
> (Matthew 5:3–4 and 10)

These verses don't go down too well with those who hawk the 'name it and claim it' prosperity doctrines of some Western churches! But it seems clear that if we want to know the kingdom, we are bound to struggle and suffer in one way or another: if not physically, then with a sense of powerlessness, with racial prejudice, with financial catastrophe, with burn-out. All these things force us to look reality squarely in the eye, and out of this experience comes living faith.

It's when our relationships and economies are crumbling that we turn towards one another and begin to love with the love of Christ. In so doing, we discover community—the same joy in sharing that I saw in those El Salvadoreans that day in 1988.

Reality was what black slaves looked at when they found themselves in Europe, America, and the Caribbean, singing songs not of fantasy freedom, but of the joyous freedom of the Spirit they found in each other and in God. They sang of the Kingdom of God because the kingdoms of this world were unbearable. For many of us a true Kingdom of God which emphasises justice is at least a diversion and at worst a threat, for the systems of this world are doing us quite well—thank you very much.

Reality was what Archbishop Romero looked at after speaking out for the poor of El Salvador for years; it was what he met when the sniper's bullet felled him in a shower of blood just as he was lifting his hands in thanksgiving for the sacrificial blood of Jesus—as he was serving at the Lord's Supper.

Reality was what ten of the twelve apostles (eleven if one includes Paul), looked at when they faced their own deaths in the church's first century—all eleven imprisoned, brutalised, tortured and murdered. All eleven...and we think we're somehow 'better' than Peter and Paul, exempt from pain?

Pain and commitments

Suffering not only develops our sense of reality, but it also clarifies our vision of the issues that really matter. The Books of Psalms and Lamentations weren't written when the prophet Jeremiah and the young man David were at a charismatic convention! Instead, David wrote many of the psalms while he was on the run from his enemy King Saul—long before he ever became king himself—and during deep regret for the moral failures of adultery and murder. Jeremiah wrote Lamentations while his beloved Jerusalem was being sacked. Today, campesinos in El Salvador and Guatemala will work for as little as two or three dollars a day if they can eke out even the barest living to feed their sick and malnourished children.

If we haven't learned to care for one another in pain and struggle, the church will be irrelevant in less than a decade. The 1991 explosion of Mount Pinatubo at least momentarily drew together rival factions in the Philippines. Seeing ruin all around him, Jeremiah warns, 'Let not the rich man boast of his riches.' The Lord says, 'Wise men should not boast in their wisdom, nor strong men of their strength, nor rich men of their wealth. If anyone wants to boast he should boast that he knows and understands me because MY LOVE IS CONSTANT AND I DO WHAT IS JUST AND RIGHT' (Jeremiah 9:23–24, NIV). We must instead expect to be purified through pain as the fire of God's fierce love burns through the shrubs and weeds of our comfortable, lackadaisical 'faith'.

Pain and questions

'My heart is crushed because my people are crushed!' (Jeremiah 8:21, GNB). Suffering not only brings us into confrontation with reality and challenges us to re-evaluate our commitments: it also makes us dance the tango with some tough questions. For too long the Christian church has sat silently when questions need to be asked. In fact, in many churches anyone who dares to ask an incisive political, social, or personal question—any question that obliges others to face reality too—is told he is being 'divisive', or 'resisting the Holy Spirit', or 'not being submissive to the church leaders'. This suppression has to stop, and many young people are in a better position to resist the conspiracy of silence than those of us who (like me, just over fifty now) see the problems less clearly.

We need to ask why the UK government's statistics on homelessness simply don't tally with the numbers on the streets on wintery nights. We need to ask where our Western banks are investing funds, and whether some of our own money is in fact being directed into arms shipments. We need to ask why (in Washington D.C., at least) convicted white men are jailed in better conditions than their black fellow prisoners. And to ask any of these questions, we need to have our eyes and ears wide open, our hearts in tune with the promptings of the Holy Spirit. In Australia, we need to ask why Aboriginals in Western Australia constitute over 40% of those jailed, whilst representing less than 2% of the population!

The vulnerable Christ

Has the church lost its vulnerability and become an unassailable, monolithic structure, more concerned with keeping 'undesirables' out than opening its arms to a suffering world? Then the church has lost its mandate. The church's vulnerability is surely one reflection of Christ himself in Gethsemane. Christ himself is most exalted on the Cross (Philippians 2:7–9). He made himself of NO reputation...took on the form of a slave...endured the Cross...THEREFORE GOD HAS GIVEN HIM A NAME WHICH IS ABOVE EVERY NAME. We can't afford to sanitise and prettify what happened at Gethsemane and Calvary by contenting ourselves with 'warm fuzzies' and mushy sentimentality. Since Jesus is the Way, there is no other way of journeying with him but in pain.

We need not, however, be silent in our sorrows. Like Jesus, we can cry out against them. Out of that pain comes prophecy.

2

Pretence or Prophecy?

When you fall in love, the first thing you want to do is tell the whole world about it. Love and joy bubble up from deep within, and they demand to be shared.

Isn't the same true of our relationship with Jesus? When we first meet him, when our illusions about ourselves are first shattered by the loving, forgiving look on his face, when we first know his healing—we want to tell others about our experiences. As we all discover, however, we can share nothing with others unless we are first willing to share their pain. We can't function like *Encyclopaedia Britannica* reps, Avon ladies, or double glazing salespeople—'selling' the gospel like some kind of consumer product and then walking away, quite uninvolved; no one would be convinced for a moment!

What this means, then, is that before we earn the right to speak of our faith we must enter into the dreams, struggles, hopes, fears, and anguish of the culture or group with whom we want to share the gospel. At no time in history has any truly prophetic word come from a position of exalted comfort, detachment, or shallow peace. *Prophecy comes from pain.* In fact, the test of whether I am a biblical, godly evangelist has nothing to do with my bank balance or my social status (or even how many people have been converted through my ministry). It has everything to do with this base-line question: if I preached the whole gospel of Christ, would my life be in danger in Beijing or Central America? Or is my gospel so watered down, so full of Western comfort that it offers no challenge and offends no one—neither here nor in places of anguish? Would my social standing be at risk in the boardrooms and social clubs of the West?

Remember Martin Luther King wasn't killed in Cambodia or East Timor or in any place we usually associate with injustice and human atrocity. He was killed in Memphis, in comfortable suburban America. This was because he was preaching the good news that gave hope to an oppressed people while at the same time causing people in power to tremble. Similarly, John the Baptiser was not killed by marauding desert nomads; he was killed by a covetous old man and his illicit wife who lived in a palace. John's sharp words and smelly animal skins were an offence in their ears and nostrils; they knew that John in all his uncompromising poverty and unattractiveness was far more powerful than they in their sumptuous splendour—and they were afraid.

Who, me, a prophet?

Many Christians would rather fade into wallpaper when their friends start talking about real prophecy. Like so many things in the Scriptures (and in our relationship with God generally), prophecy makes us uneasy. And it's meant to. It is worth noting that most Biblical prophecy—Amos, Isaiah, Jeremiah, Ezekiel, etc—is not titillating titbits about Jesus' second coming, but trenchant analysis of the social and moral corruption of the self-indulgence and indifference of the day. I'll never forget the shock I got when I suddenly understood a very familiar verse in John's Gospel in a fresh way:

The wind blows wherever it pleases. You hear its sound,

but you cannot tell where it comes from nor where it is
going. So it is with everyone born of the Spirit.

(John 3:8, NIV)

For years I had thought Jesus was talking here about
the free movement of the Holy Spirit. 'You never know
where the Spirit is going to strike next,' I used to tell
myself. But one day it dawned on me that Jesus wasn't
talking about the Spirit; he was speaking of people born of
the Spirit! This revelation shook me considerably, especially as I began to recall the boringly predictable
behaviour of most conservative Christians...as well as
their equally boring and predictable 'far left' counterparts!
Both camps, of course, are locked into an agenda dictated
by an ideology which, in the case of the Christians, has
God's signature forged on it. I knew then that I couldn't
go on worrying too much about what anyone thought of
me and my faith. They could write me off as 'weird',
'radical', or 'unorthodox'—whatever words they might
want to use—but if Christ had a claim on me, it was time
to stand up and be counted. Jesus never said to anyone,
'Go in peace, your orthodoxy has made you whole.'
Instead, he said, 'Go in peace, your faith has made you
whole' (see Matthew 9:22).

Because prophecy is born of pain, it is bound to be
radical and discomforting. Why is it, then, that we get so
caught up in our cosy little lifestyles that we don't fully
hear the stories of and about Jesus. 'Oh, I've heard it all
before,' we say, shrugging, and walking away. Well, if
that's our attitude, we haven't heard Jesus' stories at all.

This may not be exclusively our fault. Many people
have been brought up on the version of Scriptures written
in Jacobean or Shakespearean English. Such language
may be artistic, poetic, and beautiful, but it puts up a
barrier between us and God. How much harder for him to
speak to us through hundreds of years of changed and still
changing language!

Just as one example, try reading Mark 5:1–20 in a modern version. It's the dramatic story of Jesus healing a demon-possessed man, where John is recounting what happened in Gentile country (near a Roman garrison)— even though he's writing for Jews. (The early church abandoned the holy languages of Hebrew and Aramaic to spread the word in a vernacular version of pagan Greek. They forsook Jerusalem and planted the message in Rome, Corinth and Ephesus.)

Here's a man living in tombs and caves, screaming day and night and cutting himself with stones. Everything in the story shouts 'unclean' to the Jews who are reading. The wild man is living amongst the dead—a horrific and filthy image with which to begin any story, especially for a Jew. Not only that but that man is tormented by demons—unclean demons as well. Furthermore, Jesus drives the evil spirits into a nearby herd of pigs! For the Jewish audience, this story has all the elements of a sensational film: pigs, tombs, chains, madman, spirits, Gentile country; a real horror story for the religious purists! And it doesn't end there, for as soon as the man is healed, clothed and in his right mind again, offering to follow his new Saviour, Jesus simply tells him to stay where he is and remain among his own people; he is not to opt out among the clean, nice people, but stay where he is in the place of foreign Roman domination and godlessness, to prophesy to those people who are in pain. Is this the 'gentle Jesus meek and mild' of our childhood understanding? Or is this radical, prophetic ministry?

Entering the desert

Prophetic work and prophetic stories like these come as we strip away the thin veneer of civilisation. Whether or not we're conscious of it, we hide behind layers of pretence so that we can avoid admitting to our vulnerability, our fears, our shortcomings.

We fool ourselves that if we're going to offer anything of our faith to those outside Christ's kingdom, we somehow have to be more than human. But when there's a crisis in our lives, all we've been hiding re-emerges and we long for a fresh start and for relationships in which we can be ourselves and stop wearing masks. I have, in my lounge, a makeshift flywire painted mask, used by students in the days of the Nicaraguan revolution against the US backed Contras. Without a mask, students were photographed, identified, tortured and murdered by the death squads. Our fears in the comfortable West give rise to other less obvious masks.

God always wants to give us that fresh start, to be at the centre of healing relationships. To do this for us, he may call us into situations where all the 'props' of our lives are washed away; where we struggle financially, emotionally, physically and socially; where there is nothing left to distract us from the sheer grace of God, and finally we have to see the reality of who and where we are. Of course that's painful, but what makes us think that we're going to get a 'better deal' in our Christian lives than Jesus or John?

Many people refer to those times in life as 'the wilderness experience', or as the mystics called it, 'the dark night of the soul'. We certainly shouldn't be surprised to find ourselves in such a wilderness. It was in the desert that Elijah heard his call; it was in the desert that Moses confronted his own murderous spirit and repented; it was in the desert that the Children of Israel wandered for as many years as it took them to learn to depend utterly on God; it was in the desert that John preached the coming kingdom; it was in the desert that Christ's calling as God's Son was tested; it was in the desert that the early church fathers sought and met God.

People who have lived in or travelled through the desert make a variety of observations about it: that it's overpowering and daunting; that it's breathtakingly beautiful, yet lonely. But one observation common to all seems to be that the desert clarifies and sharpens our vision of who and where we are as human beings. The peace, the cleanliness, the intense beauty of rocky wildernesses or apricot dunes, the velvety darkness of a night sky pricked with stars so clear and near you can almost touch them, the pure air—all these things give desert wanderers the impression of a place that, far from being dead or sterile, is pregnant with reality. Many people return from the desert—as did those I've already mentioned—changed, challenged, on their mettle.

If we are walking with Jesus, we will all eventually go through some kind of wilderness. We will feel frightened and naked, vulnerable and perhaps even desperate. We will feel we have lost our power, our possessions—and not only material possessions, but the spiritual 'riches' we have accumulated for ourselves. We will feel *deserted*! But, in the end, we will face our own emptiness; we will face the human inadequacy of all the structures and relationships we have built up in our lives, and we will, like the Old Testament prophets before us, say 'The Lord is all I have.' Without that experience of desert, we have little to say to our contemporaries; we cannot be prophets. Without an experience of weeping, how can we hope to comfort those who mourn? Jeremiah wrote, 'Great is Thy faithfulness,' giving inspiration for the writing of one of the most loved of all hymns, when he emerged from an almost manic-depressive period of utter loneliness and dereliction (Lamentations 3).

Biblical prophecy

The prophecies of the Bible were inspired more by suffering than by anything else. Salvation has come to us through suffering, so how can we expect to escape sharing in Christ's sufferings? As Christians, many of us are biblically illiterate. We need, for a start, to become fully acquainted with the prophets, and if we've never read them before, we'll be in for some surprises. The Old Testament prophets teach us that today's wimpish pie-in-the-sky gospel has no substance or basis in the Scriptures. Even people who consider themselves faithful in studying the Bible are shocked when they hear its contents proclaimed properly.

No one who is truly biblical is locked into a particular tradition—be it evangelical, Pentecostal, or liberal. But those who are not truly biblical, regardless of the tag they wear to identify themselves, often react violently when they hear real biblical prophecy.

I experienced this truth for myself a few years ago when there was a fight in Coober Pedy, South Australia, over some land famed for its rich opal mines. Supposedly Australia has laws against racial segregation and discrimination, but racism still goes on across Australia. For example, in Port Augusta (on the south coast of South Australia), at 4 o'clock every afternoon an iron grille is lowered between the white and Aboriginal sides of one pub I know. On one side, the floor is carpeted, and meals are served. On the other (which according to Australian law isn't there at all), Aboriginals drink at a bar where there's no carpet and no food is served. The iron grate separating the two like prison bars is erected between white and black sections in the afternoon as the aborigines begin to drift in.

While on a mission in Coober Pedy, I investigated the arguments between different Aboriginal tribes and local whites. I discovered that a vicious rumour had been circulated by local Christians. In the north-western part of South Australia, in the middle of the desert, was an opal-rich area that was being given to the local Pitjandjara tribe. Rumour had it that other Aborigines in this area would be driven out or ritually murdered once the Pit-jandjaras got the land. Worse still, the stories claimed, this new territory would extend as far as the Ayer Highway in the Northern Territory, thus effectively slicing Australia in two. The rumours were utterly unfounded. It was conjectured that there would eventually be a border guarded by men with fixed bayonets—all taking part in some sort of hideous subversive Communist plot. These rumours had even gone as far as the Australian session of the Congress on World Evangelization.

I challenged some of my Christian Aboriginal friends in Coober Pedy. 'Why did you let that tale be told?' I asked. One of my friends admitted he knew there was no substance in it, and it became clear that whites unhappy about the land being settled by these tribes had circulated the story among whites and Aborigines alike until many people both believed and were terrified of the outcome of those tribes' presence on that land.

I could not keep silent. I began to speak out against all those who had concocted the fabrications in the first place and brought things to such a fever pitch. I'm sorry to say that two Christians, one of whom represented a government department in Coober Pedy, took me aside after I had preached on the injustices done.

'Young man,' one of the Christians said. 'If I were you, I wouldn't come around these parts and talk like that, because there are many mine shafts around this town, and more than one person has already disappeared down those shafts.'

So much for Christian brotherhood in the face of biblical truth-telling! Simply prophesy against material greed and injustice, and watch 'godly' people turn violent!

It was the same for Jesus, who healed many on the Sabbath—an offense to the Jews of his day. He came one day to Bethesda, a spa in Jerusalem, and there healed a paralysed man, much to the dismay of the devout Jews.

The Pharisees, the text tells us, were prepared to co-operate with their despised political enemies, the Herodians, who had collaborated with the Roman Empire, and 'they made plans to kill Jesus' (Mark 3:1–6).

> Now there is in Jerusalem near the Sheep Gate a pool, which in Aramaic is called Bethesda and which is surrounded by five covered colonnades. Here a great number of disabled people used to lie—the blind, the lame, the paralysed—and they waited for the moving of the waters. From time to time an angel of the Lord would come down and stir up the waters. The first one into the pool after each such disturbance would be cured of whatever disease he had. One who was there had been an invalid for thirty-eight years.... Jesus said to him, 'Get up! Pick up your mat and walk.' At once the man was cured.... So, because Jesus was doing these things on the Sabbath, the Jews persecuted him.
>
> (John 5:1–5; 8–9; 16, NIV)

I often think of this pool and of what happened there. No healing could take place unless the waters were troubled. No healing could take place unless feathers were ruffled. The same will be true of us: we will have to disturb the waters around us—especially the stagnant ones!—if we are to be prophetic servants of Jesus.

Prophets and heroes

Prophets, then, are ordinary people who have suffered ordinary human pain and who know the Scriptures well enough to speak about them with conviction and sincerity—reluctant and even violent as the hearers may be. Perhaps it will help us to see ourselves more clearly in the role of prophets if we know more about what makes a true prophet...and also what warns us of a false prophet. 'Watch out for false prophets. They come to you in sheeps' clothing, but inwardly they are ferocious wolves' (Matthew 7:15).

Flawed, yet fully alive

First, we need to dispense with the idea that prophets are holier than we are, somehow more than human. We are wrong to expect prophets to be cartoon figures like Batman or Wonder Woman, cardboard cutouts who never make an error of judgement, whose resolve never wavers, whose strength is unflagging, whose insight is instantaneous. We seem to want heroes who are perfect! In Australia and Britain, when leaders are proved imperfect, we tear them to shreds in the press and dump them on the rubbish heap of history; in America some pretend they are perfect after all! Both those reactions are unworthy, unintelligent, and unrealistic. Prophets are not like technicolour heroes who leap tall buildings with a single bound. We do not need heroes who are perfect; we need heroes whose lives substantially make a contribution to what is right, what is godly, and what is good.

The true prophet is like John the Baptiser. There he was, top of the preaching charts, with the crowds thronging to hear his gigs in the desert. Then suddenly the crowds were gone—the fan club and even the road crew leaving him for the latest star, Jesus. In no time at all he's in prison, full of confusion about what has happened and finally dying at the hands of a power-hungry woman not unlike the wife of Romania's Ceauşescu, in our own time.

The true prophet is like King David. There he was, sated with material and spiritual goodies. Then suddenly he falls in love with a pretty girl he sees bathing on a neighbouring rooftop. Murder and adultery later, he's got the girl but is stricken with remorse. His prophetic psalms speak for generations of sinners who have rediscovered God's love and mercy.

And what about Abraham, the father of our faith, on whom praise is heaped in the eleventh chapter written to the Hebrews? He was no Goody-Two-Shoes, either. Trapped by a web of lies of his own making, he's willing to let his own wife be taken and raped by other men. 'She's not my wife, you know,' he says with careless indifference. 'She's my sister.' So much for Abraham's courage!

We can't forget Joseph, either, hero of the much-vaunted technicolour dreamcoat. He wasn't always the magnanimous man who welcomed his brothers and ageing father and wept over their starvation. Before that he was a narcissistic, pompous boy, impossibly spoiled, impossible to live with and at odds with his jealous brothers.

Isn't it fascinating that the great ones of the Bible aspire to heroic and prophetic status in spite of their weaknesses and failures? An atheist once set out to discredit Christians by drawing up a list of all the failures of the saints and prophets down the ages, parading their grubby laundry for anyone to see. He published the list. One day it was answered by a Christian tract. Yes, the tract admitted, it was indeed a woeful and completely true list of all their wrongs. But what a fantastic statement of the love and grace of God that from such appalling beginnings and severe disadvantages these men and women rose above their own selfishness, greed, twisted sexuality, and failure in the past to accomplish something great and lasting for the human race. As well as being prophets, they were in fact fully human, and fully alive. Our attitudes in this era of fallen TV evangelists must be in part responsible for the public disgrace and delight of cynics since we encouraged the egoism and theatrical unreality of their floorshows. We share in the guilt of encouragement of false prophets of prosperity and power.

Can we forgive them that, and forgive ourselves the same weaknesses, knowing that God forgives us and has heroic and prophetic work for us to do? Biblical heroes were flawed—there's no doubt about it. But they were also used by God to wonderful purpose.

Committed

Despite their flaws, true prophets are committed to serving God and the poor. This has always been the case for the Jewish people particularly, because of their strong sense of identity. Jewish children have grown up since the earliest days with stories of the heroes of the faith, including the very ones we've noted as failures. They learn about being sons and daughters of Abraham, Isaac, and Jacob. They know they are travelling a path danced before them by Deborah and wept over before them by Ruth. They aren't nearly as afraid of commitment as we are.

True prophets are unafraid of being committed to service. My friend and colleague Steve Drury is a great example to me, especially since he's only too aware of my flaws! He works tirelessly for our organisation—Care and Communication Concern—doesn't complain about his work as much as I do, interfaces with everyone from the high-powered business community to the hurting people on the other end of the telephone with questions. Yet he still makes time for his own family, and he occasionally even finds time (when I'm pushed myself) to do something as mundane and humble as clean my shoes. Uninterested in the almighty dollar, he has the heart of a true servant of God—and therefore in God's eyes is a hero: 'If anyone wants to be first, he must be the very last, and the servant of all' (Mark 9:35).

True prophets do not go around proclaiming their own prophetic calling. Instead they point others to God, as did John the Baptiser:

> Now this was John's testimony when the Jews of Jerusalem sent priests and Levites to ask him who he was. He...confessed freely, 'I am not the Christ.' They asked him, 'Then who are you? Are you Elijah?' He said, 'I am not.' 'Are you the Prophet?' He answered, 'No.' Finally they said, 'Who are you? Give us an answer to take back to those who sent us. What do you say about yourself?' John

replied in the words of Isaiah the prophet, 'I am the voice of one calling in the desert, "Make straight the way for the Lord"…He is the one who comes after me, the thongs of whose sandals I am not worthy to untie.'

(John 1:19–23; 27)

John was an ordinary man with an extraordinary dream born in the desert of self-denial. It is no wonder Martin Luther King found courage in John's prophecy. In his historic Lincoln Memorial address in 1963, he announced 'I have a dream that one day "every valley shall be exalted and every hill and mountain shall be made low. The rough places will be made plain and the crooked places shall be made straight and the glory of the Lord shall be revealed and all flesh shall see it together." '

We can just imagine the mounting impatience and seething indignation of the religious people as John, in his ragged clothes, refused to push himself forward into any place of prominence by defining himself in exalted terms. It must have driven them crazy with jealousy and rage that he referred them instead to Jesus! Then he dug himself even deeper some time later as he told them (in words made blasphemously memorable by Christian weight-loss groupies in America): 'He must become greater; I must become less' (John 3:30).

It wasn't easy for John to lay aside his own claims and talk this way, and it isn't easy for us, either. How many times have we said, 'Lord, I don't care if I'm a nobody.' Time passes, and we become burned out with sitting in the backseat of life and playing the part of the servant. 'I want to be somebody,' we complain to God. But we haven't realised that if we're walking in faith with God, we need to burn on, not burn out. Like the burning bush from which Moses heard the word of the Lord, we need to go on burning for him without being consumed.

Unlike their counterparts in many other spheres, prophets and heroes of the faith today are marked by long-term commitment. Nowadays people flit from one job to another, one relationship to another. Years ago people who changed careers even once were seen as drifters, but today (so sociologists tell us) people may retrain as many as five or six times in a lifetime. What used to be seen as lack of commitment is now applauded simply as going up the ladder from one rung to the next, from one tax bracket to the next. Not that change is in itself an evil, of course; but when we confuse the ladder of success with spiritual progress, we're greatly mistaken. The true prophet gives his life to God, not just a year or two of it, and speaks words to the world that will have long-lasting if not eternal significance.

Because prophets are ordinary human beings they are also, like Jesus, very vulnerable. They do not always themselves understand what the Holy Spirit is prompting them to say to the world about issues that concern God. Their lives are therefore fraught with danger and confusion, and they are as liable to be corrupted as any other human beings. Knowing this helps us understand why those called into prophetic ministry seem at times to march to a different drum—to be like that unpredictable wind described in John's Gospel.

Vulnerable

Not only are true prophets likely to be in physical danger; they are likely to be subjected to temptation and to doubt the authenticity of their calling. John must certainly have gone through the pain of those kinds of doubts. Having testified openly about the Messiah, he then found himself languishing in Herod's dungeons. Filled with confusion, he sent some of his followers to Jesus:

> When John in prison heard what Christ was doing, he sent his disciples to ask him, 'Are you the one who was to come, or should we expect someone else?'
>
> (Matthew 11:2–3)

His certainties had turned to doubts, and Herod, who liked to sneak down to his cell and talk with him, must have known that:

> Herodias nursed a grudge against John for his exposure of her immorality and wanted to kill him. But she was not able to, because Herod feared John and protected him, knowing him to be a righteous and holy man. When Herod heard John, he was greatly puzzled; yet he liked to listen to him.
>
> (Mark 6:19–20)

Here's a lecherous old dictator who both fears and is fascinated by his prisoner, so he plays a game of cat and mouse with him. I often wonder how the preachers and prophets of today would cope with John's experiences. Would twentieth-century American, British, or Australian evangelists be able to look through the bars and see that God in his compassion might have a greater glory on the other side of the pain? Would they see that God's heart was aching for them, but that he had to leave them there because it's a real world, an evil world, where gutless tyrants exercise their wills over godly people? It used to be an honour to die for Jesus; now it's an honour to be a success for Jesus! But the true prophet sometimes lives, like John, in confusion.

False prophets

Wolves in sheep's clothing may be the stuff of children's folk tales, but we don't have to look too far to see them around us in the form of false heroes or false prophets. All but the most cynical of us look for heroic people on whom to model our lives. We do need those heroes, for they inspire us to thinking and actions we might never otherwise have contemplated. But we need heroes of a certain sort, and we need to have a balanced attitude towards them—neither blind adulation nor bitter cynicism.

Hollywood movie star Johnny Depp picked up this point when he was recently quoted in a girls' magazine. He said, 'Things are very bad when kids have to write to an actor for advice. I can't tell anybody what to do. I'm just as screwed up as the next guy' (*Dolly*, July 1991).

Cardboard cutouts

We don't need the Hollywood or Australian soap opera larger-than-life heroes, for a start. They only seduce us into the lie that success means vacuous, self-indulgent lives, where our homes look like glossy magazine covers or home decorating shop windows; where the washing is always white; the kids always smiling and obedient; money somehow rolling in while mum and dad lounge on the patio or by the pool.

Hollywood stars who project this kind of image are often featured in magazine articles that enthuse about their wonderful family life. A few weeks later, those same stars are blazing their way across the local cinema screens with foul language and violence to women. Are these the stars we want to idolise—those who are heroes of celluloid rather than substance?

Nor should we be sucked into the cult of the pop star complete with designer stubble, raunchy clothes, and seven-figure bank balances, with no regard whatever for the young people (particularly the women) who idolise them. Those are cosmetic heroes. We must search instead for musicians who have some admirable qualities, whose music is saying something prophetic that can change hearts, lives, and even national policies. Bob Dylan, for example, said recently, 'If nobody wrote any songs from this day on, the world ain't gonna suffer for it...unless someone's gonna come along with a pure heart and with something to say!'

Political prophets and heroes are rare, too. Image is all, and razzamatazz calls the shots in election campaigns—

not an agenda for the needy and the exploited. The Thatchers, Reagans, Bushes, and Majors of this world— hotly pursued by their campaign managers and publicity agents—give more attention to their appearance than they do to the substance of their policies. Ronald Reagan was a classic example of an anti-prophet, though he did have his staunch bevy of Christian supporters at the time. Somehow, because of the image he projected, they over-looked the astrology consultations and the lavish expend-iture of public monies on the refurbishment of the White House. His minders, we are told, researched the gullible but influential evangelical and charismatic sector to locate the favoured phrases and biblical quotes concerning morality and the second coming of Christ. President Reagan's addresses were cunningly prepared with the appropriate verses to buy votes. If he had harkened to the words of Jesus, rather than political analysts, he would perhaps have quoted Jesus' words to the crowds:

> When you went out to John in the desert, what did you expect to see? A man dressed up in fancy clothes? People who dress like that live in palaces...What did you go out to see? A prophet...But indeed you saw much more than a prophet.... The Kingdom of Heaven has suffered violent attacks and violent men try to seize it...When the Son of Man came, he ate and drank and everyone said...a friend of tax collectors and other outcasts. God's wisdom, how-ever, is shown to be true by its results.
>
> (Matthew 11:7–19)

The results of the era of self-indulgent presidencies has surely shown its results! Massive homelessness, child abuse, millions without health care, alarming unemploy-ment and myriads of beggars on the streets of the 'world's greatest democracy'. By contrast, from Jimmy Carter's world view has emerged the image of a rejected President, building houses for the poor, through Habitat for Humanity!

We need to ask here about the future of democracy, if all the emphasis goes on the 'sizzle' rather than the 'sausage'. And we need to see, too, that if we admire people who have sold us the sizzle of clever rhetoric, without the sausage of a compassionate social system, then we are likely to become as empty-headed and callous as they are. Can we search instead for politicians who make a genuine contribution to the human race and to the environment, rather than flaunting a parade of glitz based on money and power games?

Politicians aren't the only ones addicted to image, and technology is making the cardboard cutout (once so obviously a cartoon caricature) into a Frankenstein far more 'real', more three-dimensional. Already photographers can by use of digital computers adjust the bytes of a photograph so that an unwanted curve here or unsightly scar there can be removed to project the 'perfect' image. And within the decade, I'm told, people will be able to put on a special headset and by means of laser technology see three-dimensional holograms of people who simply aren't there. Even now it's possible for film frames or photographs of Marily Monroe to be fed into a computer in such a way that she can act out a scene with say, Sylvester Stallone on screen; as has been recently done in a Diet Coke ad featuring Elton John, Louis Armstrong, Humphrey Bogart and James Cagney.

Worse is yet to come as the pornography industry gets hold of the technology. As in the horrific vision of Aldous Huxley's *Brave New World*, porn film watchers will within a decade be able not only to see computer-formed hologram images of women from every possible angle and in every possible sexual position, but they will at the same time be able to use complementary technology to experience sexual stimulation which corresponds with the images. The ultimate invasion of privacy emerges as a new generation of sex-crazed perverts acts out rape scenes using hologram images taken from photographs of their neighbour's wife or perhaps even home movie film of her children.

False heroes and false prophets may wear sheep's clothing, but they also bear a few clear and distinguishing marks: they are greedy—for money, sex, and power; they are short-lived; they have their fifteen minutes of fame, then burn out like comets streaking across a dark sky; they make no contribution and no commitments to anything. Often they do and say outrageous and impossible things. They're punched in the face and jump right up again to deliver a knock-out blow in return. They bounce off speeding cars without a bruise to show for it. They fiddle with their big-bore hunting rifles, toss them over their shoulders, and shoot the eyes off a spider without a moment's hesitation for the recoil—and we fall for all of it! Above all, they put up a glittering facade that admits no vulnerability and no pain—and therefore no truth.

We can follow false prophets if we like, but we'll be following a fantasy. But if we dare instead to pray 'Your kingdom come', we may rise above our fantasies, and actually recognise the hope of the kingdom of God. The suffering Jesus calls us out of Tinsel-Town fantasies into his kingdom of hope, pain, change, and love. If we are indeed to follow him, we will find ourselves speaking for him out of shared suffering.

3

John the Baptiser: God's Work in People and Places

I often wonder how it is that we have taken the Bible, a volume filled with every aspect of human drama and brokenness, and somehow made it into a dead, irrelevant book. In fact it is full of life, and it offers us that life if we will open our hearts and minds to its stories. In its rich array of characters, flawed and full of doubt as well as faith, we see a mirror image of our own failures and moments of triumph. We see men and women who were fully alive to God.

The story of John the Baptiser is surely one of the most heart-rending tragedies in literature. This fragile but powerful man was a voice for God, and if we read his story carefully, we will lose some of the illusions sold to us as truth by Western anti-prophets. Concentrating on John for a while, and then on some of his spiritual predecessors and descendants, I'd like to blow away some of the myths, the illusions, that many of us have about the way God works in human lives.

John the unlikely and unbelievable

The first chapter of Luke's Gospel tells the tale. In our haste to reach the narrative of Jesus' miraculous birth, we may miss this story altogether, and in so doing miss its important message. John was a prophet of reality, born into and dying in pain. Like all the other great carriers of the Good News at the time—Jesus, Paul, Peter, and Stephen—he was a jailbird; he was given a false trial, and he was finally executed. But we need to read about his birth to understand how some of this came to be.

Act 1 opens with the account that his parents were old and wanted children desperately. Elizabeth, we're told, felt disgraced by her barrenness. This may jar for some modern readers. While in John's day childlessness was a scourge, mistakenly thought to indicate the lack of God's blessing in life, there are today thousands of young people (yuppies or dinks) choosing to have no children so that they can carry on enjoying themselves without the responsibilities of carrying on a heritage and caring for others. If ever there were a story that gave the lie to the notion that walking close to God means a smooth and prosperous life, the story of Zechariah and Elizabeth is a classic example.

Next we discover that Zechariah, John's father, was on duty in the temple on the day when the news came that was to change his life. I had read this story many times without realizing that by John's day so many men were in the priestly line that the duty roster was enormous; there was no guarantee that a priest would have the opportunity to serve in the temple, even once in a lifetime. For a godly old man and his wife, Elizabeth, this was further heartbreak in a life already filled with the disappointment of infertility. But at last, as Act 1 unfolds, Zechariah gets his moment of glory, his chance to serve God on behalf of the many worshippers who are waiting outside.

This is a story for the aged and disillusioned in this era of the idolatry of youth—'Old men shall dream dreams' of the outpouring of the Spirit, we are told by the prophet Joel. God's purposes are not necessarily the property of the young.

Those moments in the temple turned Zechariah upside

down, full of joy and wonder at being at last in the inner sanctum. Then yet another miracle broke on him; the news that his wife was to give birth to a son, John. He was not the first to be terrified by the visit of an angel messenger, and not the last. Nor was he the first to say, as Abraham and Sarah had said before him, 'How can I be sure of this?' (Luke 1:18). These cautious English words no doubt belie the searing pain, doubt, and disbelief behind them. But whatever attitude he adopted, one thing is clear: when he eventually emerged from the temple to face the people outside, he was dumbstruck.

Act 2 opens with a parallel scene from the life of Mary. Much younger, Mary had less reason to doubt the prophecy of Jesus' birth than Zechariah the birth of John. Even so, she was puzzled and amazed. Still, she surrenders herself to God's purposes and sings a song of praise for the wonder of God's care for the downtrodden. That familiar song (verses 46–55), distanced now by its Latin tag ('Magnificat') and by countless elaborate choral settings, is radically prophetic: a manifesto for the poor—the poor in spirit and the poor in substance; a testimony to the loving mercy of God on all who are in anguish.

It is into this atmosphere of disillusionment, heartbreak, weariness, and wonder that John the Baptiser is born. Through what better eyes can we view the world's pain? God intervenes by miracle into sadness and disappointment, and he raises up a man who is unafraid to speak of that loving mercy to a privileged and powercrazed society. John's voice is the voice of a radical and frightening gospel; there is nothing soft about his uncompromising stand as he addresses those who come to him for baptism.

Three times the crowds try to make do with the outward show of change, weaseling out of their response by deflecting John with the repeated question, 'What should we do then?' Three times John brings them up short with answers that require a change of heart, not only of behaviour:

> The man with two tunics should share with him who has none, and the one who has food should do the same...Don't collect any more [taxes] than you are required to...Don't extort money and don't accuse people falsely—be content with your pay.
>
> (Luke 3:11, 13, 14)

Here John is not saying to the downtrodden poor that they should be silent in the face of unjust pay for hard work. Instead he's addressing the rich, and the powerful, the tax collectors and the soldiers—in other words those in Roman Judea who held the reins of power and used them to oppress others. He is challenging them to love as God loves; to be just and merciful.

His voice, like that of other prophets, still rings true in the twentieth century. It is a threatening voice, however, and it goes against the grain of anyone who wants to stand in solidarity with power and privilege in our own era.

Old Testament prophets

John's voice is not unique in its courage. Like his father before him, John followed in a long line of men whose lives were given to God at the expense of their own safety and comfort.

Amos and Micah are among many Old Testament prophets whose words echo down through the ages to our own time. Like John, Amos was certainly no candidate for a popularity contest. His prophecies are strident, angry, and disturbing; as a result, he is often misunderstood.

I heard one televangelist a few years ago, for example, take a verse from Amos and twist it around until it meant quite the opposite of what it said. Preaching on Amos 6:1 ('Woe to you who are complacent in Zion, and to you who feel secure on Mount Samaria') and calling his sermon 'Is the tassle worth the hassle?', he commended the graduating class of young people for spending years studying for a degree, since prosperity and position were available to all who work hard! The tassle of the graduated academic mortarboard was worth the hassle for the prosperity it would earn! As I listened, it dawned on me that he wasn't advocating work on behalf of the dying in Calcutta or for AIDS victims in hospices; he was advocating the old Western work ethic whereby his listeners were supposed to work like mad for big houses and big salaries. What a far cry from Amos' words, 'As a shepherd records only two legs or an ear of a sheep that a lion has eaten, so only a few will survive of Samaria's people who now recline on luxurious couches' (Amos 3:12, GNB).

There is of course no room for the TV preacher's interpretation of Amos's words, and if we don't know that, it's time we read the Old Testament prophecies properly. Amos was not a man to mince his words. Where John called his listeners a nest of snakes, Amos used stronger words that would send many holy people today into paroxysms of horror—real hands-over-the-ears stuff:

> Hear this word, you cows of Bashan on Mount Samaria, you women who oppress the poor and crush the needy and say to your husbands, 'Bring us some drinks!'...You lie on beds inlaid with ivory and lounge on your couches. You dine on choice lambs and fattened calves...You drink wine by the bowlful and use the finest lotions, but you do not grieve over the ruin of Joseph.
>
> (Amos 4:1 and 6:4, 6)

Amos is not condemning wine nor the eating of meat, nor even the use of ivory. What he *is* condemning is the idle, self-indulgent lifestyle that is built on the backs of those who have nothing; for it is a simple principle of sociology that where a greedy few have much, the many poor have nothing. Essentially he is calling the women of

Samaria, who ignore the poor, 'fat cows'! As in his day, such proclamation is not a career move or a popularity campaign. The voice of compromise is always preferable in times of prosperity.

> You people hate anyone who challenges injustice and speaks the whole truth in court *(or in the pulpit or on TV, we might add!)* ... I know how terrible your sins are and how many crimes you have committed. You persecute good men *(and women)*, take bribes and prevent the poor from getting justice in the court. AND SO, KEEPING QUIET IN SUCH EVIL TIMES IS THE CLEVER THING TO DO!
>
> (Amos 5:10, 12–13, GNB)

God also puts strong words into the mouth of the prophet Micah. The Book of Micah is familiar to many people often because of only one verse, which foretells the birth of Jesus at Bethlehem (5:12)—a reassuring little text that rolls out of the pulpits every year at Christmas. But a closer look at the rest of the prophecies shakes the reader a little:

> Listen...you leaders...you rulers...
> Should you not know justice,
>   you who hate good and love evil;
> who tear the skin from my people
>   and the flesh from their bones;
> strip off their skin
> and break their bones in pieces...
>
> (Micah 3:1–3)

Micah's vision here is horrific: that those who ignore the needy are acting like cannibals. The scene he paints is exactly the opposite of the sacrificial love of Jesus on the Cross, giving his own body for the tearing of the world; exactly the opposite of the Lord's Supper which both commemorates that sacrifice and enacts the drama of true sharing. Given words like these, perhaps it's hardly surprising that men like Amos and Micah lived on the edge of society: marginalised, feared, mistrusted, ostracised. The message of Micah, that we are called first and foremost to 'act justly and to love mercy and to walk humbly with [our] God', is just too much for most of us to stomach.

New Testament prophets

Mary, mother of Jesus, followed in the same prophetic tradition. It's a pity that, one way or another, we've rather lost the real Mary in the baggage of our religious and cultural heritage. Catholic Christians have mystified her, made her into a simpering plaster and gilt statue, wrapped her in a pretty blue cloak, and set her at a distance from our pain. Protestant Christians, meanwhile, have fared little better. Fearing to idealise her in this way, they have gone to the other extreme and ignored her altogether. Both reactions overlook the courageous woman who mothered Jesus: a peasant girl with nowhere better to birth the Saviour than a smelly stall reserved for animals; a poor woman whose first visitors after the birth were disreputable shepherds from the fields. (Shepherds in Christ's day were viewed as gypsies are today in Europe). To find a twentieth century equivalent, it's as if God put Mary on the 70-foot Mexico City rubbish dump, breastfeeding her child in front of a gathering of homeless women and children. Many Mexican Indians have no better way of earning a living than scouring through reeking heaps of garbage for scraps of food or saleable items. We can readily see the offensiveness of locating Mary here. But this was in fact nearer to the environment in which Mary gave birth, into which God's Son was to be born than the aseptic images of our sanitized Christmas cards.

Singing her song of praise to God, she did not congratulate herself as the mother-to-be of the Saviour. She thought only of the poor and the sinful who would be lifted up by hearing that the Son of God was to be born to an insignificant teenage girl (an unmarried mother) in a backwater of Roman civilisation. Overflowing with joy and wonder, she sings of God filling the bellies of the starving. No slappy happy clappy chorus, this, but a song of delight in the justice of God to the needy.

> He has brought down rulers from their thrones
>   but has lifted up the humble.
> He has filled the hungry with good things
>   but has sent the rich away empty.
>
> (Luke 1:52–53)

Try preaching words like that in El Salvador or ghettoised Los Angeles, and see what happens! Give me Mary's song, any day, rather than an empty chorus that trumpets my own private salvation.

People often ask—as they asked John the Baptiser— what they must do to be saved. The answer can never stop at 'be born again', for conversion isn't something isolated that happens just in the soul; it's something radical that happens to an entire life. John the Beloved, probably the youngest disciple to follow Jesus, wrote prophetically about this in his letter to the early Christians:

> Here is the clear difference between God's children and the devil's children: anyone who does not do what is right or does not love his brother *(or sister)* is not God's child...This is how we know what love is: Christ gave his life for us. We too, then, ought to give our lives for our brothers *(and sisters)*. If a rich person sees his brother *(or sister)* in need yet closes his heart against his brother *(or sister)* how can he *(she)* claim that he *(she)* loves God? My children, our love should not be just words and talk; it must be true love, which shows itself in action.
>
> (1 John 3:10, 16–18, GNB)

Disturbing stuff, isn't it! If we say we love Jesus, we're called not just to care for an elite group of people who look, talk, and think as we do, but for all human beings in need.

St Paul too suffered the pain of a prophet. Beaten, shipwrecked, hated, and finally imprisoned, he followed Jesus, John the Baptiser, Mary, and John the Beloved in preaching a radical gospel, a gospel that was to change people from the inside, not the outside:

> Love must be sincere…Be devoted to one another in brotherly *(and sisterly)* love. Honour one another above yourselves…. Share with God's people in need. Practise hospitality. Bless those who persecute you; bless and do not curse. Rejoice with those who rejoice; mourn with those who mourn…Do not be proud, but be willing to associate with people of low position.
>
> (Romans 12:9–16)

Lest someone seek to interpret such words as applying only to our fellow believers, Galatians 6:10 instructs us to do good to all humanity! Jesus is described in 10:38 as the one who went about doing good—no wonder Peter describes Him as the JUST ONE. In Ephesians 2:10 Paul says our new birth in Christ is expressly for the purpose of enabling us to do good works.

Prophets whom God has raised up through the ages are those who have been bold enough to suffer the persecutions and still love; suffer the pains and still prophesy. And there have been very many such men and women, in many places.

Prophets in Britain and Australia

John Wesley was one of the flawed but completely committed prophets of the British Isles. His ministry was sacrificial, costing him more than many people realise. Because his marriage didn't work out, we smart Alecs, a couple of centuries later, can sit in easy judgment on him and make our armchair pronouncements. But I wouldn't dare guess what went wrong for Wesley, even though I've read volume after volume about his life.

Whatever happened in Wesley's marriage, he is the one who gets the credit for lighting the first fires of freedom in the hearts of men and women who wanted to see an end to slavery at a time when many saw no wrong in it. He wrote passionate tracts denouncing slavery, even to the point of losing one of his dearest mentors (Whitfield), who disagreed with him on the issue, justifying his use of slave labour in building orphanages in Georgia.

Twelve years before the anti-slavery moment was founded, Wesley wrote a savage tract of 70 or so pages attacking the system. When a young adolescent called William Wilberforce read it, he was forever changed. Wesley's final religious act while on his deathbed was the writing of a letter to Wilberforce to persevere in his work against slavery at whatever cost. More than eighty years old, weary from the quarter of a million miles he had ridden on horseback to preach the gospel of Jesus, Wesley still had the strength left to pass the prophetic mantle to his own Elisha; and Wilberforce certainly took it from him.

On one of those days everyone thinks of as typically British—murky sky and cold drizzle—I stood not long ago on the banks of the River Humber. I had been walking with some friends along the edge of that silt-laden river, and the tide was going out so that we could see the muddy flats of the riverbed. We paused and stood outside the home of Wilberforce. Seeing the river through his eyes, we could almost imagine the hot indignation he must have felt over the years as he watched some of the estimated 50,000,000 human beings who were dragged out of Africa on cargo ships to become slaves in England and the Americas. Fifty million people torn from their homes and their cultures to underwrite the economy of already greedy nations.

Despite the general acceptance of slavery, William Wilberforce could not keep silent. Like Wesley before him, he spoke out against the way the slaves were treated— worse than anyone would now think of treating an animal—rape, torture, beating, starvation, and mutilation…in so-called Christian civilization! So he fearlessly championed the cause of slaves in a society that met his outrage with blank surprise, scorn, or indifference. 'Fight on!' Wesley had said to him, '[against] this inexorable trade in human flesh'—and fight he did—right until he died. Although Wilberforce knew he had the necessary votes to win, he did not live to see the passing of the parliamentary bill that was to free the slaves, because it cleared the House about two weeks after he died—but the slaves were free at last. The prophetic bravery of Wesley and Wilberforce was not wasted. While physical slavery ended in the USA in the 1860's, economic and political forms of slavery continued until a century later, and motivated another prophetic voice, that of Martin Luther King, likewise inspired by Jesus Christ, to give his historic speech in Washington D.C.:

> So let freedom ring from the prodigious hilltops of New Hampshire; let freedom ring from the mighty mountains of New York; let freedom ring from the heightening Alleghenies of Pennsylvania; let freedom ring from the snow-capped Rockies of Colorado; let freedom ring from the curvaceous slopes of California. But not only that. Let freedom ring from Stone Mountain of Georgia; let freedom ring from Lookout Mountain of Tennessee; let freedom ring from every hill and molehill of Mississippi. From every mountainside, let freedom ring.
>
> And when this happens, and when we allow freedom to ring, when we let it ring from every village and every hamlet, from every state and every city, we will be able to speed up that day when all of God's children, black men

and white men, Jews and gentiles, Protestants and Catholics will be able to join hands and sing in the words of the old Negro spiritual: 'Free at last. Free at last. Thank God Almighty, we are free at last.'

While Wesley, Wilberforce and King are well known, other prophets are rarely heard of outside their own country. Australian Donald Mackay was one such. A big man in height (6′ 3″), Don was humble in spirit. He and his wife were Methodists, warm, loving, and Spirit-filled people. For all his quiet strength, however, Don was not one to keep quiet when he discovered that young children in the neighbouring town of Griffith, New South Wales, were being used as couriers for drug-runners.

Don had noticed that gate after gate leading into nearby fields was bolted in a particularly careful manner. After watching and investigating for a while, he realised that the crop all these fields had in common was marijuana. Immediately he went public; he called in the NSW police and spoke to politicians in the highest echelons of government. Word was out, and Don's days were numbered.

A little while later he stopped in town one Saturday night to buy a bottle of wine for a meal at home. There in the car park outside the shops he was struck down by hitmen who knew exactly whom they were looking for. While shoppers passed unawares, his blood was spilled in the car park. The hitmen left no trace of Don except the bloodied smears of his hands that had slid down the door of the car as he collapsed. He had paid the ultimate price of prophetic proclamation.

Prophecy in America

Friends who know me well enough to tease say that I never have a good word to say for Americans. In fact this isn't true at all! Certain Americans tower head and shoulders above their contemporaries. Abraham Lincoln comes to mind immediately, but there are many in our own time whose voices have rung out in prophecy over Western greed and injustice.

The voice of prophecy against racism by no means died with Wesley and Wilberforce; as previously mentioned Martin Luther King delivered one of the most inspired, magnificent and artistic speeches given this century when he spoke to a huge crowd in Washington D.C. on August 28, 1963. 'I have a dream,' he cried, and soon thousands were dreaming with him of freedom from oppression and from poverty for black Americans. 'You must have tough minds and tender hearts,' he told the civil rights marchers who flocked to his call. Five years later he was dead—shot by a sniper's bullet as he stood on a motel balcony in Memphis. The people who heard him speak couldn't stand the truth he told. Today economic poverty, instituted in political Machiavellian structures and majority self-interest, still challenges the vast majority of disenfranchised black Americans. A new voice is urgently needed in the wake of the 1992 Los Angeles uprisings.

And what of the Kennedy brothers? Tragically and seriously flawed, these men nevertheless stirred a nation from its slumbering post-war complacency. John Kennedy caught the imagination and hearts of a whole generation of idealistic youngsters, weary of 'we've-always-done-it-that-way, son' politicians. Young, Catholic, he changed the American presidency forever... and he too was gunned down.

Bobby Kennedy, a man some say of greater integrity than his brother, seemingly also destined for the White House, stood up heroically against the Mafia and was prepared to walk the streets to canvas for the poor. He campaigned against racism and drew America's attention to the plight of Latin Americans. Whatever the smut merchants may say about his sexual conduct, he challenged his world and left his marks of goodness on it. But like his brother, he died at the business end of a gun.

History won't forget the Kennedys, but it may well dismiss another prophetic president with much greater integrity and clear Christian commitment: Jimmy Carter. History has already been unkind to this man, buried him (though not yet literally) because, like John the Baptiser, he has refused to follow the trend of the time and substitute rhetoric for reality. Voters threw him out in favour of one who slashed social services, dramatically increasing the numbers of the homeless. Yet Carter was a man who could not stand by while 75% of the people of Washington D.C., the nation's capital—nearly all of them black—lived in poverty. He was brave enough to say there had to be a change, and to set about doing something about urban poverty.

He is still working for the underprivileged. While other ex-Presidents (including Nixon, who was forced to resign over illegal wiretappings in the Democrats' campaign headquarters) thread their way back and forth across the nation earning as much as $200,000 per speech, Carter—the first president not only to say that he was born again, not only to continue his lifelong church attendance and Baptist Sunday school teaching, but also to dare say that national security is less important than obedience to God's commands—puts on grubby overalls and goes to work: building houses for the poor in Nicaragua, in Chicago, and in the Deep South. Since he left office the former head of the most prestigious 'corporation' on Earth has bloodied his thumbnails and got splinters in his hands putting up housing for the poor, working with Habitat for Humanity. This is the same man who as president cancelled all aid to El Salvador until there was a full investigation into the brutal rape and murder of American nuns—an order his successor countermanded in the first week of his office. Hear these words from the modern prophetic voice of Jimmy Carter (quoted from *Target 1992* No. 2):

The greatest discrimination of all is the discrimination by the rich against the poor. This troubles me very much because I am one of the rich, and so are all of you.

We have a home in which to live. We have food to eat. We have a job. We have self-respect. We have a modicum of education. We have security. We have the belief that if we make a decision, at least in our own lives, it will make a difference.

But there are many people who have none of these things—not a single one—these are the poor. And quite often we Christians build around ourselves a shell of not deliberate but inadvertent isolation.

We have a natural inclination to be with people just like us in a homogenous society where we are not disturbed in our security and relative wealth.

He then goes on to make some extraordinary and unexpected comparisons between the US and the third world of today.

In our own country we have a higher proportion of our citizens in prison than any other nation on earth. A baby is more likely to survive today if it's born in Bangladesh than if it's born in Harlem...There is a sense that in this great democracy, perhaps the pre-eminent democracy on earth, we are not able to care for our next door neighbour.

Prophecy in Central America

The kingdom of God will never prevail through guns, but through the love of God. This means that as Christians we are all caught between our hearts, which cry out to us to stand up for the poor, and our knowledge of the Scriptures, which teaches us to love our enemies. That dilemma is what makes the Christian faith so full of paradox; that dilemma is what has driven radical thinkers in Central America to be so 'revolutionary', to formulate what is known as liberation theology and to act on it. Like all 'single issue' theologies it has its inherent dangers and extravagances, but it has opened up the debate concerning the application of faith to politics and the real world.

It is said that this theology is a mixture of Marxism and Christianity. That sounds frightening, until we realise that most of Western Christianity is a mixture of capitalism and Christianity—it's just that we're too short-sighted to see our own cultural biases and so dismiss a theology foreign to us as having no merit at all.

If you want at least to see another perspective from the Latin struggle, I recommend a book by Gustavo Gutierrez, the man who wrote the first major volume on this theology, called *A Theology of Liberation* (SCM, 1974). Another book of his—prophetic and inspiring and one that expands considerably on his original thinking and which seeks to find more balance between the justice issues and the search for spirituality—is *We Drink from Our Own Wells* (SCM, 1984). This book looks at our need to find spirituality not just by some kind of trip into the inside of our heads, but to see it rooted in campaigns for the poor and for the plight of all in third world countries.

Perhaps the man most famous for his quiet teaching and living out of an evangelical form of theology for the poor was Archbishop Oscar Romero, Catholic Archbishop of San Salvador. Here was a man chosen because he was thought to be politically harmless: known as a shy, inoffensive, short, unimpressive little man. 'We've got a few rebellious priests who get us into trouble with the CIA,' the authorities thought, 'but this one won't cause trouble.' They certainly underestimated him! He called his Catholic hearers to discover the Protestant doctrine of conversion and called all Catholics and Protestants to live the gospel in all aspects of our existence.

Romero was a man who knew the gospel and who knew its costs. As he saw some of his people speaking out against the brutal tyranny of a vicious regime fuelled by Western 'aid'; as he learned of the injustice, exploitation and arms dealing in that little country; and as he discovered that some of them were murdered or 'disappeared' for their prophetic stance, he began—like others before him—to march to a different drumbeat from that of church and state hierarchies.

Every week he preached more and more boldly over the local radio station. Sunday by Sunday he asked around to find out who was missing from the congregation, and why; and he encouraged the people in his congregation to speak about relatives who had been murdered during the week. A lay minister from the congregation would read aloud the names of all the missing and murdered, and after each name, as in a liturgy, the people would cry out 'Presente!' Their shout of triumph and defiance was to commend each one to God: 'Jesus, we present to you the martyrs who have died for peace and for believing in your gospel, seeking to live it out in this torn country.' And then someone would also read out the name of the military officer who had ordered the killings.

One day this Archbishop went too far. On the radio he preached about true conversion, about the work of the Holy Spirit to change hearts and lives, and about the significance of the gospel in work for reconciliation between the warring factions in El Salvador. He ended his sermon with an appeal to all soldiers who heard it to lay down their weapons. In substance he said:

> In the name of Jesus, I command you, put down your weapons. And if your commanding officers tell you to do something that Jesus tells you not to do, you are under no obligation to obey your commanding officer in the army. In the name of Jesus, the killing must stop. Lay down your weapons in the name of Jesus.
>
> (Taken from a transcript of his address.)

The right-wing fanatics shot Romero a few days later during the Wednesday Lord's Supper in a little local chapel. The story has become well known now, but it bears repeating. He lifted the chalice and warned that just as Jesus had died for us and shed his blood, so we must be prepared to die for one another. Barely had he so challenged the audience than the assassin's bullet tore into him and left him drowning in his own blood at the foot of the altar. Kneeling at that same altar a few years ago, I wondered how much we understand the heart of the Gospel, till we have seen it through the eyes of its martyrs.

Archbishop Romero was like John the Baptiser, a voice of one crying in the wilderness. In his own flesh he lived and died the words he had once spoken. It was Jesus who asked, 'Which of the prophets have you not stoned?' Romero suffered for his correct assumption that

> We cannot segregate God's word from the historical reality in which it is proclaimed. That would not be God's word and the Bible would be no more than a pious history book in our library. But it is God's word because it enlightens and contrasts with and repudiates what is going on in today's world.
>
> (*The Church Is All of You: Thoughts of Archbishop Oscar Romero*
> [Winston Press, 1984])

Prophecy in India

So far we have looked at prophets who were known as Christians. We would be arrogant to assume, however, that God cannot speak through those who do not—or say they do not—know him.

India is a country rich in ancient spiritual traditions, so perhaps it is not surprising that India would produce 'voices crying in the wilderness' like Gandhi. He did not acknowledge Jesus as Saviour, or even as Lord, but— modelling some of his philosophies on Jesus's Sermon at the Mount—he stood for change in a society which was riddled with twisted legalism and oppressed by the caste system. Like John the baptist and Isaiah, Gandhi longed to see mountains levelled and rough places made plain. He too died in his quest for peace.

Mother Teresa certainly professes Christ. Perhaps she will never die like Romero from gunfire, but she will surely die from her untiring efforts for the poor and unlovely in Calcutta. All the destitute are welcomed by Mother Teresa and her fellow Sisters of Charity. Westerners who come to visit and work with her for a while shed the trappings of Western achievement in both material and spiritual terms and are permitted to address each other only by Christian names. No 'reverends' or 'fathers' or 'doctors' here!

And when she is not holding a dying leper in her arms or rescuing unwanted babies from the Calcutta rubbish tips, Mother Teresa—at least until recently—has travelled the world to draw others' attention to the needs of the hungry and the greed and indifference of countries who have allowed such unjustice to go on unchallenged. She is a living illustration of the folly of deliberately misinterpreting the verse 'You will always have the poor among you' (John 12:8) as if it meant, 'The poor will always be around—so what?' Rather, she proves that the work of feeding and caring for the poor will always go on, and that Christians should be in the midst of them caring for their needs. And when we are, we discover what it means to have the kingdom of God in our midst.

> Once, having been asked by the Pharisees when the Kingdom of God would come, Jesus replied, 'The Kingdom of God does not come with your careful observation, nor will people say, "Here it is" or "There it is" because the Kingdom of God is in the midst of you.'
>
> (Luke 17:20–21)

Wherever Christ is—there is the Kingdom. And wherever the Spirit and activities of Christ are expressed in the activities of his followers—there we see a glimpse of the Kingdom and will of God—on earth as it is in Heaven!

Mother Teresa is brave and prophetic enough to embody the meaning of the Incarnation and the Eucharist in her work: she gives people on the edge of life and society a taste of 'God with us, Emmanuel'.

Prophecy in South Africa

Desmond Tutu, like Oscar Romero, received official recognition by being 'raised' to an archbishopric. But he has more in common with Romero than that, for he has taken seriously the bidding that 'He who wants to be the first, he must be the very last, and the servant of all' (Mark 9:35). Risking his life repeatedly and suffering the taunts of those who would brand him 'communist', he has championed the cause of the poor and spoken out against the racist injustice that has kept South African blacks oppressed for so long. He dared to warn blacks and whites alike that if there was no change in South Africa there would be a bloodshed more terrible than anything so far seen in that unhappy land.

Like the prophet Deborah of old, Tutu danced in praise to God when Nelson Mandela was freed from prison in 1990. Imprisoned in his mid 40's for his radical actions and words on behalf of those who endured the indignity and pain of apartheid, Mandela had remained incarcerated—like so many before him—until he was an old man. I often thought during those years that if Jesus himself had preached in twentieth-century South Africa he would have been in the same cell as Mandela. Or perhaps not in the same cell...one a Jew, and the other a black...at best they might have been able only to talk to each other through the bars.

Prophecy and non-believers

At this point in our walk through 'the great cloud of witnesses', or, as Americans would put it, 'God's hall of fame' some of you will panic and jump to the next chapter. But what makes us think, as Christians, that we have a monopoly on the truth?—especially since God himself acknowledges in Scripture the gift he has given those who do not know him to speak his truth to the world. If His followers would not speak out, Jesus said—upon His triumphal entry to Jerusalem—the stones would cry out.

God is not beneath the dignity of using even an ass to speak prophecy—and I don't mean the two-legged variety! We read in the book of Numbers (Chapter 22) that when the prophet Balaam refused to obey God and return to Moab to see Balak, the king, it was the donkey on whom Balaam rode who obeyed God and warned Balaam to go back. Three times risking Balaam's fury, his beatings and his sword, she was given the gift of speech so that Balaam would see the folly of his obstinacy.

Nor is it beneath God's dignity to use a pagan king to prophesy over and liberate his chosen people. King Cyrus of Persia (550-529 BC) knew the agony of the Hebrew people taken captive years before by the Babylonians. He discovered, too, that the Hebrew prophet Isaiah had foretold his actions in prophecies written for Judah at some time between 740 BC and 680 BC—roughly two hundred years before his reign! Famed for his clear-headed administration based on recognition of cultural diversity within his huge empire rather than on military might, Cyrus (so the historian Josephus tells us) was filled with 'an earnest desire and ambition...to fulfil what was written' (Antiquities, XI, 1, 2). Though he reigned over what was then the largest empire known in history, stretching from India to Ethiopia, he showed mercy to the Hebrews and was called by God 'my servant':

> I am the Lord...
> who says of Cyrus, 'He is my shepherd
>   and I will accomplish all I please;
>   he will say of Jerusalem, "Let it be rebuilt,"
>   and of the temple, "Let its foundations be laid" '...
> 'This is what the Lord says to his anointed,
>   to Cyrus, whose right hand I take hold of
> to subdue nations before him
>   and to strip kings of their armour...
> So that you may know that I am the Lord,
>   the God of Israel, who summons you by name...
> though you do not acknowledge me.'
>
>   (Isaiah 44:24, 28; 45:1, 3–4)

Down the ages others who like Cyrus did not know God have taken up the cause of the oppressed. Whatever we may think of the classic Marxist ideas about economics, we don't deny that because Marx was talking and writing about oppression, he was in a way close to the heart of the prophets and of Jesus. (It is well worth reading Anthony Campolo's outstanding paperback, *Partly Right* (Word Publishers), for a much more extreme development of this thesis—particularly as regards Marx). Marx saw that the rich get richer and the poor get prison and he wanted to change that. We miss something if we put him in a neat little box labelled 'communist' and are blind to the way Marx raised the social conscience of a generation who wanted freedom from the tyranny of injustice. Tragically, in the absence of a more balanced, committed Christian response, atheistic political ideologies hijacked the revolt against Czarist tyranny and Russian poverty.

We could say the same of an Australian prime minister, Gough Whitlam, who called himself an atheist. In spite of this tag, and in spite of what it might have cost him politically, he took a lead from Christians working for Wycliffe Bible Translators' Summer Institute of Linguistics. He sat in the dust with aboriginal tribal people protesting against the way the Australian bureaucracy was taking away the rights and opportunities of Aborigines to use their mother tongue. He insisted upon the use of tribal languages in government negotiations with those whose culture was still intact.

Yet another prophet, in a strange way to my mind, is the American film director and actor Woody Allen. Woody portrays himself as an insecure man. Sometimes he reminds me of Moses—Moses ran away into the wilderness because he had failed to pull off a social justice coup, had been caught out, and had ended up killing the equivalent of an Egyptian policeman. In spite of what modern preachers have said, however, in the wilderness of Midian he wasn't doing a sort of Bible college internship; he was actually looking after sheep! Even with a serious identity crisis, Moses was capable of caring for a flock of dumb sheep!

Woody Allen works out of the wildernesses of Manhattan. Somehow, this man (who would never claim to have had a personal encounter with God) has learned that he can be secure about getting on with his art, getting on with his cinematic search for meaning and humanity without the need for the acclamation that the world gives. This is why he appears free from the need for fame, free from the need for Oscars and Academy Awards for his films; if he wins them, he doesn't go to receive them but is likely to be found playing his clarinet in a local club, just as if the award night wasn't even happening.

Woody Allen is a necessary voice, a gift of God to twentieth-century culture, because he is willing, in a position of immense vulnerability, to confront tough questions both privately and publicly and to look as absurd as can be. He is a fool for God, whether he knows it or not. Compared with preachers who parrot the same old phrases over and over again, Allen—who dares look at human pain, dares laugh at it, dares make us engage with it—seems sometimes to sound strangely prophetic. His movies shout to the world that whether we have faith or not, unless we have an honest, real foundation for our lives inwardly, psychologically and spiritually, we are just playing games and all we do is meaningless.

In this age when the enlightenment of the scientific era has given us freedom without meaning, it is sadly the non-Christian artist who is most likely to stand in the flame of human alienation and pain. While Christians are willing to say with writer Graham Greene that 'It needed a God to die for the half-hearted and the corrupt' *(The Power and the Glory)*, we need also to see that every generation needs the prophetic insights of God's prophets, whether they know themselves to be so, or not. We need the Martin Luther Kings who say, 'I've been to the mountain top. I have a dream.' We need Oscar Romeros who preach self-sacrifice and die the death of a martyr for the poor. We need William Wilberforces who stand against the tide of their time and speak for justice for oppressed peoples. We need Woody Allens whose humanity articulates the weeping voices of those in emotional pain.

Most of all we need Christ-centred prophets and heroes who mean what they say when they pray 'Thy Kingdom come, Thy will be done *on earth as it is in heaven.*'

4

Music: Quick Fix, or Prophetic Spirit?

Music is as liable to misunderstanding, criticism and attack as any other artform, especially as so much of it arises from human pain. We tend to think of music in terms of celebration and joy—which it often is; but even when it is joyful, it has often been written as an escape from the pain of its composers. As we have seen, suffering is a purifying influence in human experience. Without it, some of our greatest music would never have been composed. Musicians are in some ways the artistic nerve ends of a dying culture; they are often troubled people, and we can't afford to simplistically dismiss their music for what we see as their aberrant behaviour. We need to extend to them the kind of mercy and justice that the prophet Micah wrote of:

> What does the Lord require of you?
> To act justly and to love mercy
>   and to walk humbly with your God.

(Micah 8:6)

Written out of pain

Some of the first compositions which later were used in Handel's Messiah, for example, were written at a time when Handel was in prison for not paying his debts. As he finished the work, he had a vision of angels ascending and descending into Christ's glory. The Hallelujah chorus that concludes the piece is a sublime expression of hope in the midst of adversity; it was certainly not written in the middle of a charismatic convention where Handel could have felt the warm fuzzies about some kind of cerebral 'faith'. It was written out of pain.

Tchaikovsky was a man a long way from writing 'Hallelujahs'. This great man was emotionally tormented and confused by his bi-sexuality. Even so, or perhaps even because of that anguish, he wrote some of the most lyrical and poignant music in the European canon: not only the great symphonies with which so many listeners are familiar, but also the sacred music. I always remind conservative Christians about Tchaikovsky when they start grumbling about the 'loose morals' of contemporary musicians, begging for more of the classics! (Often what they're complaining about when they talk about rock music is that they don't understand or feel at home with it, so they assume all sorts of spiritual judgements based on their emotions.)

Beethoven, too, lived with the pain of encroaching and eventual deafness. He poured out his music in the hope that he could outrun this disability—and failed. In his last will and testament he wrote sadly of the pain he had felt during his life over the gossip and speculation about his character, over the gossiping people who had called him an egotistical, stuck-up man. How could he tell them, he wrote, that he could hear little or nothing of what they were saying? How could he admit his deafness, for fear that his musical career would be over before he was ready to surrender it?

Classical composers were not alone in writing out of pain. When the church discovers the blues and jazz—and all their derivatives—it will have discovered the broken heart of humanity and so be one step closer to offering healing. Wounded musicians like Charlie 'Bird' Parker, for instance, wrote and played extraordinary jazz. Barely a teenager, Charlie 'Bird' Parker became hooked on purple hearts and other drugs. His addiction was one way for him of coping with the pain of a chaotic family life; his father, an alcoholic, was stabbed to death by a prostitute when Charlie was a young man. As Charlie grew up, he changed relationships the way most people change socks. By the time he died, still only a relatively young man himself, all his internal organs had been ruined by his lifestyle.

Yet no one has produced more innovative music for a saxophone than he did. When white jazz musicians came along and borrowed the style of their black counterparts, Charlie was one of the first black musicians to make the break into be-bop and experiment with new forms. His music speaks for a generation of young black artists from whom white musicians filched musical ideas, and whose music they commercialised and from which they made their fortunes.

The vulnerability of music

Secular music is a contentious issue for many Christians. This is where some people get sidetracked by 'straining out a gnat but swallowing a camel' (Matthew 23:24). Writing to his little brother in faith, Timothy, Paul warned him about foolish controversies over petty issues:

> If anyone teaches false doctrine and does not agree to the sound instruction of our Lord Jesus Christ and to godly teaching, he *(she)* is conceited and understands nothing. He *(she)* has an unhealthy interest in controversies and quarrels about words which result in envy, strife, malicious talk, evil suspicions and constant friction between people of corrupt mind.
>
> (1 Timothy 6:3–5)

The church needs to hear those words today; we waste

more time arguing over cultural minutae than we spend responding to the cry for help from needy people—including the musicians themselves. Evangelicals and charismatics on both sides of the Atlantic are unhealthily hung up with mindless debates about whether a certain drumbeat is satanic, or whether a group has recorded a subliminal message backwards in a song to encourage its listeners to satanic worship.

Two young Christians once came to me with a U2 record they said had been back-masked with the words 'Satan is king'. I had spent considerable time with Bono, Larry and the Edge, enough to know where those U2 men were in their world-views, and I knew they would never subscribe to any such message, let alone record it. The girls played the album to me over and over again on a tape recorder, and I was utterly unable to hear the back-masking they were convinced was there. New in the faith, these two girls ended up more obsessed with what their minister had said about the evils of rock music than with discovering the full joys and opportunities of their new relationship with Jesus.

While silly arguments over back-masking throw the baby out with the bathwater, we cannot pretend, however, that there aren't problems with music. It's a powerful art form, one that reaches more deeply into the human spirit than naked language: and because of this it is open to corruption.

Rock group CHAPTERHOUSE's Steve Patman observes, 'Of all the arts, music is the only one that can affect you immediately, without you having to read anything into it. Not like looking at a painting and seeing what it does to you, or reading a book and having to analyse what is said.' 'So, therefore,' he says, 'I feel we—as musicians—are dealing with the most powerful artform.' This is a sobering thought indeed when considering the comments of Bob Timmins, therapist to US based actors and rock stars, who tells us that: 'A lot of the reason guys get into rock in the first place is because they don't want people telling them what to do.'

Some ways in which music gets twisted are blatantly obvious, but others less so; Christians aren't guiltless in their own use of music, not by any means.

Like preachers and prophets, musicians are vulnerable to the seduction of the crowd. What an amazing thing, especially for someone who may be insecure to start with, to look into that sea of adoring faces and know that what I preach or sing has deep significance in so many lives. Because the crowd tends to make gods of its stars, the pressure is always there. Public performers—whether TV preachers or rock musicians—can too easily be seduced by this kind of excitement into an addiction to power, a megalomania that differs only from Hitler's thirst for power in degree—not in kind.

John the Baptiser knew that thirst for power, and no doubt he had a healthy respect for it. No wonder he replied steadfastly to all enquiries about his own role that he was only a 'voice', and that the One who would come after him was greater.

Knowing this, our response should be two-fold: as fans we should be aware that musicians are only human beings, and as such can actually be ruined by our idolatry. (Nor are Christian musicians exempt! I am embarrassed sometimes when I remember mediocre Christian musicians strutting about as if they were kings, treating their fans like adoring slaves; showing no compassion or sense of real fellowship at all.) And as performers we should be aware of our own susceptibilities in this regard, placing our art back in the hands of the Giver rather than claiming the glory for ourselves.

Both as fans and as performers there is another question to ask, and that's to do with the quality of our music. Technology has advanced so far now that studios can take a third-rate voice and make it sound terrific. It no longer matters whether a singer is gifted, whether she or he sings with any intelligence, or with any compassion for the audience. Making money and making noise to drown the pain—these have become the ultimate.

As Barry McGuire of 'Eve of Destruction' fame once put it (*Contemporary Christian Music Magazine*, June 1988):

> So record companies sometimes must choose between people who minister and people who sell records. The person who really sells records is gonna win every time because the company has to keep the cash flow going or they are out of business.

Quality isn't just to do with sound, either, but with the meaning and impact of the lyrics. The richest people on earth now are *not* those who produce goods or services of lasting value, but those who produce three-minute wonders which sometimes make a mockery of the word 'music'. And a whole generation—particularly of young girls—idolises them. The same young people who in clear-headed moments work against and object to the horrors of sexual abuse and violence to women are those who make heroes of the George Michaels and Madonnas of this world. George Michael screams 'I want your sex,' and Madonna begs for 'hanky panky' with 'someone mean and bossy'. Music like this depersonalises human beings and robs relationships between men and women of the capacity for respect, compassion, and intelligence.

Neither uncritical adulation nor downright dismissal will help us respond to music constructively. Somehow we seem to have lost our ability to think through the issues of faith in the real world. In our anaemic, unthinking way we ignore music that has prophetic and creative value and satisfy ourselves instead with the pathetic stuff exuding from television and tapes; we strain out the gnats of silly quibbles and swallow the camels of lack-lustre, half-inspired music that deadens our senses and turns us into irrelevant spectators of life.

Even as Christians we miss out on real music. Sentimental choruses that repeat mindlessly the wonder of God's love for me, me, me are viewed as preferable to music that makes us think, makes us shift in our seats and ask, 'Hey, does this mean I've actually got to change?' Lost in self-interest, we forget that Christ is Lord over all things, including rock music, and we act as if we are offering those around us tickets to a long queue at the celestial Wembley Stadium, waiting for the 'forever sacred' concert in the sky with Jesus as compère.

As Easterners often remind Westerners, we've been given two ears and only one mouth. It's time we stopped blotting out the cries of the hurting world by turning up the praise volume at inappropriate times. We sing with the prophet Habakkuk:

> Though the fig tree does not bud
>   and there are no grapes on the vines,
> though the olive crop fails
>   and the fields produce no food,
> though there are no sheep in the pen
>   and no cattle in the stalls,
> yet I will rejoice in the Lord,
> I will be joyful in God my Saviour.
>
> (Habakkuk 3:17–18)

Do we know what we're singing? We're singing words from the end of Habakkuk's short book of prophecy, but we haven't first gone through the journey of pain that he endured. In this way our charismatic celebrations become empty and shallow, as adept at drowning the world's pain as anything more risqué from the charts. We're dwelling in the land of spiritual warm fuzzies, the comfort zone that shuts out pain; we're increasing the ecstatic experience. Above all, we're getting ourselves a spiritual fix.

Music as analgesic

Years ago a Christian woman I knew challenged my love of rock music, specifically my enthusiasm for Bob Dylan, whose work I had loved since before he professed Christianity. 'How can you like Dylan so much?—he's a godless man, and he's like all the others now, into drugs,' she asked.

Teasing her, because I knew how much she liked Tchaikovsky, I replied, 'How can you like Tchaikovsky? He was demented; he was sick.' That went right over her head; she couldn't see her own inconsistency. But her question raises an important issue: why so many musicians have been caught in the dark world of self-destruction.

Once again we come back to the place of pain. Musicians' vision is honed and clarified by their creativity; they, at least, can't successfully blank out the pain, as can many who think and see less clearly. Instead they express it. But when the music is going badly, when the audience doesn't want to know, when the fans stop buying the albums, and when the lights go down at the end of the concert, the pain is still there staring them in the face.

As British-born stress management expert Roy Masters explained in 'Why stars self-destruct' (*New Dimensions*, September 1990):

> But for the majority of us, experimenting and suffering through false fulfilments and eventually becoming dissatisfied can lead to the discovery of what went wrong. Pain has a good side; it teaches us to discern the false from the real, and develops in us a strong basis of true belief from which to reject false love and fulfilment as the wrong answers they are. The answer to not living right can never be found in fame, glory, or any other substitute, but in discovering what it means to live properly, rooted in the patient endurance, forgiveness, and inner confidence that suffering can teach.

There are at least three reasons why musicians—or anyone—take analgesics whether it be sexual promiscuity, chemical addiction or addiction to crowds. Again, Roy Masters comments:

> For a moment, put yourself in Elvis Presley's or Marilyn Monroe's shoes and imagine what it would be like to be worshipped by millions. There you are on stage, with millions of adoring and screaming fans. You feel wonderful. As the late Janis Joplin, considered one of the greatest white female blues singers of her generation, described stardom: 'That 40 or 50 minutes I'm out there, that's when it happens for me. It's like a hundred orgasms with somebody you love...I live for that one hour on stage. I love being a star more than life itself.' That transcendent moment on stage feels as though it will last forever.
>
> Sounds pretty great, doesn't it? But there's a major downside.
>
> Everybody loves to be loved. yet there is something strangely negative and destructive about being unconditionally loved by everyone, being constantly reminded that you are wonderful and can do no wrong.
>
> What happens when you're worshipped? Ask any pretty woman who has experienced the unsolicited attention of lustful men. While it may be flattering and exhilarating to her ego, she experiences a mysterious downside, a feeling of being abused, along with a horrible contempt toward those men. This reaction leads to great emptiness, guilt, and depression—a love/hate for being worshipped.

Addicts want to escape into another world where they hope the pain will be less; they want to find oblivion by maintaining their success while reducing the pain of loneliness in the crowd and popularity's demands. They may want to energise themselves, psyche themselves up for the next road show, the next gig in a stream of one-night stands and empty hotel rooms, devoid of real love. The drugs are just another fix when the music doesn't work;

another 'trip' to ease the loneliness, the longing for love, intimacy and stability.

It's this aching void that haunts so much rock and roll now. We can sit in judgement on it, or we can hear the cry of the voice in the wilderness address it with meaning and sensitivity. We can turn up the volume of praise meetings, or we can write and sing songs that have as much bite as 'Ship of Fools' (by World Party, in the charts in 1987), a song clearly appealing to Western nations to stop living the kind of lifestyle that is leading our planet into self-destruction. While there are many examples of perverse and even satanic verse in the music charts, there are hundreds of songs which express prophetic, passionate insight into the human condition.

Foreigner cry out in anguish, 'I want to know what love is.' Van Halen ask, 'Give me truth, give me something real.' Faith No More plead, 'My life is falling to pieces, somebody put me together.' Supertramp cry, 'Won't you please, please tell me who I am?' Michael Jackson proclaims, 'If you want to be my brother, it don't matter if you're black or white.'

It's time we challenged one another and stopped accepting music as anything less than the wonderful expression of the potential that God has given us to help the human heart to understanding and creative fulfilment. It's time we turned our back on so-called Christian lyrics that could have come from a kindergarten songbook—no matter how clever the music is—and went for spiritual meat, so that we can grow up in Christ without false analgesic quasi-spiritual props.

Music as gift

All gifts of God have the potential to be distorted. The preacher can turn his gift to power-mongering and manipulation. The administrator can turn his gift to ruthless efficiency or ambition at the expense of Christian compassion. The artist can turn his gift to self-indulgent pleasure seeking. Music, as we can see, has an equal capacity to be corrupted, and its composers are as frail as any other 'prophets' who carry a painful message. But that doesn't mean that we can reject the message or the messenger.

Music frees us

When our worship of God centres exclusively on the pulpit and on the words that come out of it, we are missing something. On stage a musician gets carried along not only by the unfolding of the musical themes and ideas in his head, but also by the underlying feeling in his heart. It doesn't matter whether he's a concert pianist playing Tchaikovsky with such passion that he is almost treating his piano stool like a trampoline, or whether he's a rock singer leaping across the platform and smashing his guitar. In either case, the music has set the performer free in some way: free to forget self. Of course that freedom can turn from liberty to license, but the important issue here is that it's the music itself that has given the freedom. Music releases us from cerebral closed-mindedness and opens us to realities we may have been trying to shut out. While there is a cerebral rational side to life and faith there is equally a God-ordained and appropriate sensuality as expressed in the erotic, but monogamous, poetry of the famous Song of Solomon. Spirituality, sensuality and intellectuality are meant to be balanced friends.

Music communicates truth and anger

Those who argue over back-masking, or over painful and destructive lifestyles of some musicians, have missed the point. The two girls who worried about U2's album did not see that U2's music might be a useful vehicle for bringing the gospel to their friends. In the end, it doesn't matter so much what a song says backwards as what it says forwards! People can debate as much as they like about whether or not Bruce Cockburn is a Christian. (I'm sure he is, but whether or not—his lyrics are stunning), but too often those debates lead to shallow judgements that eventually have driven some musicians away from the tenuous footholds of faith they have begun to establish. It really doesn't matter one iota (except to them) whether Jackson Browne, Bono Vox or Whitney Houston are Christians. Christ does not need the endorsement of any celebrities—particularly those with a tenuous, often fragile relationship to the ordinary lives of the masses.

Jackson Browne's music is filled with the desire for dreams to be fulfilled. On his album *The Pretender* he was honest enough to write and sing about the meaning of true patriotism. By conventional definitions, Browne is no patriot; he is too critical of America's stars and stripes. But to my mind his prophetic songs, some of which have made me weep more than once, say more about the real meaning of patriotism than any number of speeches from the White House, during (for example) the Gulf War. The true patriot is one who can confront the weakness in his nation, name it, and call for justice and mercy. Browne's music affirms the Old Testament proverb—'Justice makes a nation great' (Proverbs 14:34—the Hebrew word rendered 'righteousness' is more accurately translated 'justice').

Rock music, unlike much modern preaching, doesn't pull any punches. It thumps out its message with pulsating energy and moral rage. Mahler's fifth symphony, the best of blues and jazz, the songs of Bono on U2 albums—all these challenge Christian assumptions that preaching is the only way to reach people.

The arts are the nerve ends of a culture and music is the cry of ecstasy and pain when the culture is delighted, demented, damaged or destructing. If you care about your fellow human beings—listen to their cries of musical pleasure or pain.

Music as prophecy

In the end, much as we may not like this thought, it doesn't matter where truth comes from; all truth is God's truth, and (as we saw in Chapter 3) pagans can speak prophetic truth as well as Christians. Someone once said that if forced to choose they would rather run into the arms of truth than into the arms of Jesus because if they ran into the arms of truth they would find themselves in the arms of Jesus anyway. (Sometimes the carefully constructed Jesus of our self-centred culture is a dressed-up effigy of the one who said 'I am the truth'.)

Christians sometimes act as if truth were a private thing, as if it had our names on and no one else's. But that's not how God, who so loved the whole of creation that he sent his only Son to die for it, views truth. We need to remember this as we recall some of the rock musicians whose truth has burned into society over the past few years. We need to remember this when we're tempted to sit in our rocking chairs and measure the length of musicians' hair, thus stumbling over external signals of the counterculture and missing the internal truth of the message. It is significant that St Paul in Acts 17:28 quotes a love poem to Zeus—a pagan Greek god—to make a point he could well have made from a biblical verse. But it spoke the vernacular language of their hearts—and he wished to touch their hearts.

U2 and Bono

Bono is surely one of the world's top musicians. His work is fuelled by Irish Celtic spirituality, of which some Christians are unjustifiably afraid because it seems foreign to them; his songs are full of spiritual anger, a searching hunger for God and an understanding of how hard it is to grow as a Christian. None of this of course makes Bono a mature theologian, nor would he claim to be; in fact, when Bono and the others are asked directly about their faith, they often have trouble articulating it. But that doesn't mean that they don't know and love God; it just means that they are still struggling in their faith, and that they are as full of confusion and flaws as most other artists. And God doesn't necessarily want U2 to go into the studio and record a string of religious songs—they don't need to, because what they've already recorded does challenge many to think about the Christian faith. Bono's words 'I still haven't found what I'm looking for' could well be a theme song for a whole generation of young people.

Once when I was talking to Bono he said something I'll never forget. Paraphrasing Jesus' words about the kingdom of God and his work in it, he said that the principal criterion for judging the worth of someone's ministry is whether or not the work brings healing and wholeness to others. I suspect that Bono was thinking of the answer Jesus sent to John the Baptiser in prison about his Messiahship:

> 'Go back and report to John what you have seen and heard: The blind receive sight, the lame walk, those who have leprosy are cured, the deaf hear, the dead are raised, and the good news is preached to the poor.'
>
> (Luke 7:22)

One song of Bono's (one of many) that calls for a response from mind and soul is 'Sunday Bloody Sunday' from their early *War* album. Recalling Jesus' words 'Father forgive them, for they know not what they do,' Bono addresses the pain of children's suffering in places of war; how Jesus has died not only for them, but for those of us who should be working for peace:

> Broken bottles under children's feet
> Bodies strewn across a dead-end street...
> Wipe your tears away...

Claim the victory Jesus won
On Sunday, bloody Sunday.

Listening, we can't help realising that thugs and bikers aren't the only ones perpetrating violence today; the Pentagon needs as much forgiveness, as do Christians who countenance outrages against children by looking the other way...and that's what makes this kind of song such a threat. U2 are unique in not only criticising accepted social norms (including war!) but in proposing alternatives. So we need to pray for Bono and U2; they're in the front line, and they're bound to be on the receiving end of a few bombshells—many of them thrown by envious Christians! I have felt a bit out of touch of late and must admit to some intuitive concerns about both public pronouncements and rumoured events concerning the guys. But I love them and only pray their extremely dangerous spot at the top will not make them slaves to money, sex and power—the nemesis of fame and fortune.

Midnight Oil

In Australia, Midnight Oil have made an impact as strong as that of U2. Many sections of the USA have responded with almost fanatic approval of this hard hitting, uncompromising band. Their manager, Gary Morris (possibly our most celebrated rock manager) and lead singer Peter Garrett, have clearly, publicly declared their faith and commitment to many vital issues in a way almost unequalled in the more secular circuit, at least in OZ. Commitment to Aboriginal justice, human rights, values, personal integrity, have marked their management, lifestyles and music. There has never been the personal posturing, strutting, loose moral self-aggrandisement which has marked so many others—even professedly Christian rock stars. I simply revel in the joyous reality that these guys are saying something and courageously challenging the powers of greed and indifference in our day.

Cliff Richard

Obviously, one cannot ignore Cliff Richard, whose persona is so clearly Christian, whose life has been so transparently clean and good as well as generous to the poor through Tear Fund and other agencies. His professional, energetic, brilliant performances remain decade after decade an example of faith and excellence. In terms of his music, I have to say it doesn't cook for me with the poetic brilliance or sheer heart energy, moral rage and pathos of Bruce Cockburn. Cliff is a brilliant entertainer—Bruce is an incendiary lone John the Baptist.

Bruce Cockburn

Here's a musician who writes and sings with anger in his voice, and that may make some of us draw away—though mistakenly. He has a passion for the poor of Central America, and he is subtle but quick to speak out about his faith. His music is indirect about the faith that informs it—another (unjustifiable) reason for Christian suspicion of his motives. He has gone on record at least once saying that he doesn't feel he should 'sell' his faith in the songs; that evangelism in the sugar-coated pill of rock music is not for him. Instead, he says, he is committed to expressing things that he sees and hears, things that move him. His songs may not name Jesus (some do), but they certainly proclaim him for those who want to listen. For any who want to feel the prophetic heart of Amos to music I recommend Bruce's song—'It's a Stolen Land' in *Radium Rain*.

Bruce Springsteen

Bruce Springsteen writes, like so many of his contemporaries, of the lack of fulfilment in human life. His two 1970s albums *Born to Run* and *Darkness on the Edge of Town* articulate the hunger of the human heart for heaven in a world full of broken dreams and empty landscapes. He never quite seems to offer answers to the questions his songs raise, stopping just short of Christian commitment himself, but at least he's asking the questions.

Hearing the cry

From the 1960s onwards, rock music has galvanised Western culture. In so many quarters, for the discerning, seeking concerned ear there are prophetic strains to be heard—sometimes in the flow of what appears to be clear commitment to faith as in Van Morrison's double album *Hymns to the Silence*; and sometimes in the searing heat and sometimes confused theology of Tracy Chapman. But it's there! My deepest frustration in the arts is the fact that, when I search for honesty, pain, righteous anger, profound insight and deep moral commitment to vital issues for humanity—it's usually a so-called secular group or artist who meets my need. There are some real exceptions—not the least being my Welsh mate, Martyn Joseph, or Garth Hewitt, Adrian Snell and Ben Okafor; those whose music and whose friendship have given me hope for a time when we will cease being in the sad state of the Israelites, whose expression of creative art had so expired, they were forced to hire pagan Philistines to create artifacts for worship. It has been a creative thrill to be assisted in pubs, bars and other totally secular venues by Australian artists such as Rob Timms, Glass Canoe and many others whose names will mean little to most readers of this book, but whose existence, passion and relevance may be signs of a long overdue revival of the arts as a prophetic nerve end to an anguished world in a creative renewing alternative way.

When Mick Jagger gyrated his hips and screamed into the microphone 'I can't get no satisfaction,' he wasn't just singing about sex. Even though he may never have understood it in these terms, he was singing about the anguish and alienation and ache of young people for the God whose name they may not know. He was also singing in the language of those same young people. When John Lennon sadly reflected on the demise of the counter-culture age of Aquarius, he said 'The dream is over...we've got to get down to so-called reality.' I think this applies to the church as well as to the world.

Are Christians going to sit on the sidelines and listen to musicians who really do know how to communicate passion, pain, and prophetic moral outrage? Are Christians only going to offer as an alternative the kind of platitudinous choruses that Jesus would surely weep over? Are we going to content ourselves with spiritual analgesics that are as dangerous as any hard drug? Or are we going to hear the cry of pain and do something about it? Rock and roll—any music in fact—demands a response beyond reflection or idolatry.

5

Greed and Grace

Then he said to them, 'Watch out! Be on your guard against all kinds of greed; a man's life does not consist in the abundance of his possessions.' And he told them this parable: 'The ground of a certain rich man produced a good crop. He thought to himself, "What shall I do? I have no place to store my crops." Then he said, 'This is what I'll do. I will tear down my barns and build bigger ones, and there I will store all my grain and my goods. And I'll say to myself, 'You have plenty of good things laid up for many years. Take life easy; eat, drink and be merry.' " But God said to him, "You fool! This very night your life will be demanded from you. Then who will get what you have prepared for yourself?" This is how it will be for anyone who stores up things for himself but is not rich towards God.'

(Luke 12:15–21)

Greed—covetousness, as it used to be called—is as old as human beings. It is what drives us to acquire more than we need. We bring nothing into this world and take nothing out, so if we have enough food and clothes we should be happy; and if we have more than that we should be generous and ecstatic! But if we are set on having more and more—always at the expense of others, then—no matter how much we kid ourselves—we're falling into the trap of the rich fool in Jesus' story.

Frequently those to whom the Old Testament prophets wrote and preached were greedy: for power, women, land, and possessions. They raped and plundered and pillaged without mercy, and their greed was not confined to the battlefield; as we have seen, much of it was the kind of greed familiar to Westerners today: the greed of the comfort zone, ignoring all pleas from the deprived and downtrodden.

The Roman Empire was no better. Until Constantine, Roman Emperors couldn't have cared a fig whether they were going to heaven. Some of them even had themselves declared gods, giving themselves the deeds of title to anything and everything under their sway. The only Roman imperial concern was that the militaristic, materialistic empire should advance and prosper without opposition.

No wonder early Christians were such a threat! The Roman authorities discovered that increasing numbers of soldiers in their over-stretched army were following the man Jesus, who preached 'love your enemies' and would no longer take up arms against 'enemies'. The Greek Menology claims that early in the second century AD, ten thousand soldiers in the legions of Armenia were executed at one time. Many of these men were crucified, all of them executed for putting the Kingdom of God above the might of Rome. A further 1,000 were exiled. Nothing could be allowed to stand in the way of the Roman thirst for money and land.

Sadly, centuries later, the church carried on much as did the empire. In the Middle Ages and afterwards it was the notorious sale of indulgences, pardons, and prayers for the sick and dead that lined church coffers, purchased church jewelry, and housed church pontiffs like princes. Today it is the sale of televangelists' prayers and holy hardware (trinkets often made in the third world) that builds exclusive Christian leisure and holiday complexes as well as hospitals and colleges that house Christian

people, young and old, in palatial comfort. The unbelievable self-indulgence of at least six major US televangelists
has severely discredited evangelism over just five short
years of the eighties and nineties.

The many faces of greed

Jesus was of course quite familiar with human greed as he
entered his teaching ministry. He knew, and knows still,
our habit of intellectualising faith until we can't see any
more what his life and words have to do with our own
lives. We say we follow Jesus, but in practice what we
mean is that we think we understand the doctrines of St
Paul rather better than most other people! But time and
time and time again, Jesus said, 'Follow me!' Jesus knew,
and knows still, that we aren't just greedy for material
wealth; if we call ourselves Christians we may also be
greedy in a more insidious way for spiritual power and
prestige. Both spell destruction to us.

His story of the rich fool is one we'd love to sweep under
the carpet. We don't want to walk with him along the
painful road of generosity and care for others. We'd rather
work ourselves to death, then say we've earned our 'little
nest egg and plan to enjoy it, thanks very much'. In
reality, as heart-attack statistics show for so many high-
flying executives these days, we're not likely to enjoy much
of anything except a shortened life. We'd rather flatten
ourselves serving on church committees and youth leadership teams, then say we've earned our 'trip to the
Wembley Stadium in the sky' and don't need to hear
about this painful kind of discipleship and self-giving.

In Jesus' time the Judean lifestyle did not separate the
world of the political, social, moral, and spiritual. When
we bring our compartmentalised views to bear on the
story of the rich fool, therefore, we're in danger of missing
the point. God is the ruler of everything. Hence, God is the
God of economics as well as of the spirit. God hasn't given

us a set of guidelines for sexual conduct and left us in the dark about how to use money. Instead he has told us we must be completely just in our use of money—and presumably, also, in our use of all gifts and abilities.

But what has happened in Western 'entrepreneurial' culture? Capitalism has gone mad: the poorer you are, the higher proportion of your earnings is paid in tax. The more you earn, the more you can manipulate the system to avoid or even defraud governments of taxes that could be used to help the poor. And in many Western churches, money is stored or spent on gorgeous silver that has to be locked up Monday to Saturday 'just in case those nasty people outside might want to come in and steal what we've got'.

I know one Australian, for instance, who is a doctor earning a million Australian dollars each year. He goes about boasting that he has never paid any taxes. But are we purveyors of the good news when we tell the poor to tighten their belts yet again and cough up the next round of tax increases, while large corporations are squandering monies on frenetic publicity campaigns built on (and still expanding) profits that are made on the backs of the poor?

In my country, believers and unbelievers alike in electrical, plumbing and building businesses request cash payments to avoid taxation. They have their four-wheel drives, beach houses, extensions, etc, on incomes they declare to be on the poverty line. They want the police to protect them but don't want to contribute through taxes to their wages. The blatant greed and subsequent dishonesty lurks equally in the skirts of Christian and non-Christian tradesmen, fueling a destructive, hidden black economy.

The story of the rich fool is not aimed at people struggling to make ends meet, a moral tale designed to extort more from already depleted purses. Rather, this story is aimed at those who are self-righteous and smug in their material and spiritual riches. The Pharisees would have groaned and covered their ears in horror and dismay or (if they were honest) shame. What about us? Are we storing up material and spiritual riches without any regard for those who have none? Are we counting not just our money but our prayer meetings and Scripture meditations, relying on these to win us salvation, when justice is what is required? If so—hear the Word of the Lord—Isaiah 58:3, 6, 7, 9–10; Jeremiah 22:13–17; Zechariah 7:8–12; Micah 6:6, 8:

> The people ask, 'Why should we fast if the LORD never notices? Why should we go without food if he pays no attention?'
>
> The LORD says to them, 'The truth is that at the same time you fast, you pursue your own interests and oppress your workers.'
>
> 'The kind of fasting I want is this: Remove the chains of oppression and the yoke of injustice, and let the oppressed go free. Share your food with the hungry and open your homes to the homeless poor. Give clothes to those who have nothing to wear, and do not refuse to help your own relatives...
>
> 'When you pray, I will answer you. When you call to me, I will respond.
>
> 'If you put an end to oppression, to every gesture of contempt, and to every evil word; if you give food to the hungry and satisfy those who are in need, then the darkness around you will turn to the brightness of noon.'
>
> (Isaiah 58:3, 6, 7, 9, 10)

Doomed is the man who builds
    his house by injustice
  and enlarges it by
    dishonesty;
who makes his countrymen
    work for nothing
  and does not pay their
    wages.
Doomed is the man who says

'I will build myself a
   mansion
   with spacious rooms
   upstairs.'
So he puts windows in his
      house,
   panels it with cedar,
   and paints it red.
Does it make you a better king
   if you build houses of cedar
   finer than those of others?
Your father enjoyed a full life.
   He was always just and fair
   and he prospered in
      everything he did.
He gave the poor a fair trial,
   and all went well with him.
That is what it means to know
      the Lord.
But you can only see your
      selfish interests;
   you kill the innocent
   and violently oppress your
      people.
The Lord has spoken.

(Jeremiah 22:13–17)

The Lord gave this message to Zechariah: 'Long ago I
gave these commands to my people: "You must see that
justice is done, and must show kindness and mercy to one
another. Do not oppress widows, orphans, foreigners who
live among you, or anyone else in need. And do not plan
ways of harming one another."

'But my people stubbornly refused to listen. They
closed their minds and made their hearts as hard as rock.'
(Zechariah 7:8–12)

What shall I bring to the Lord, the God of heaven, when I
come to worship him? Shall I bring the best calves to burn
as offerings to him?...No, the Lord has told us what is

good. What he requires of us is this: to do what is just, to
show constant love, and to live in humble fellowship with
our God.

(Micah 6:6, 8)

Idolatry

Greed is a subtle form of idolatry—one sin most of us
think is limited to 'pagans' who kneel before carved or
painted statues. We need to look again at ourselves and
see that we are all greedy, especially in the West. We
ignore Jesus' simple but terrifying words that it is more
difficult for rich people to be saved than for 'a camel to go
through the eye of a needle' (Matthew 19:24). We are
always trying to defend greed and dress it up, hide it,
rationalise it in all its ugliness and viciousness, and so we
evade Paul's instruction that we 'put to death...greed,
which is idolatry' (Colossians 3:5).

While suburban executives and their well-heeled wives
in Washington DC, the capital of the US, drink their
morning orange juice in their well-appointed breakfast
rooms and plan the next weekend party or cruise, black
young men of 18 and 19 are queueing at the Church of the
Saviour for free soup. And those same kids may have
earned $1,000 the week before for playing 'Spot the Cop'
for dealers—then blow it all on crack themselves. When
asked by a friend of mine what they would be doing if they
weren't in crack rings, they shrugged and said they'd be
rioting.

American or not, can we afford to say these problems
have nothing to do with us? Or do we need to ask questions about the imbalances and inequities of a system so
corrupt that such situations can take root and flourish at
all? We are caught up in the greed ourselves, and it only
takes Christmas to remind us; then we paw through lavish
piles of useless, self-indulgent and (in the end) unwanted
luxury items looking for the 'perfect gift' for the person
who already has everything, forgetting that in Central

America and parts of the South Pacific no one ever has such a burdensome problem.

Consumerism

Greed is by no means the exclusive province of Americans. Australian and British people are no different. In the 1960s two young men caught up in the angry-young-man counter-culture started a magazine called *OZ*. In an attempt to shake people out of their cultural and social lethargy, the two publishers made outrageous cover designs depicting for example crude scenes in church, or the Mona Lisa with bared breasts. The public response was pavlovian: outrage on all sides—but the publishers were laughing all the way to the bank.

By the late 1980s, these men were very prosperous indeed. By then they were looking back on their passionate efforts to change the world and trivialising them. They discovered that money did not in itself bring relief from the pain of what they saw around them. One of them returned to his childhood Christian roots, and the other became a workaholic—desperate for a sense of doing something, anything, to get a fix against the pain of fear of death and non-being. But interestingly—one of these men—Richard Neville, somewhat of an Arts icon in our Australian secular society, recently attacked pornography and movie violence as too dangerous in our currently dying culture.

Another story may illustrate how, when the chips are down, the very rich are in fact completely absurd in lifestyle and impoverished in ethics. I heard the newspaper tycoon Randolph Hearst wanted a particular painting for his art collection. 'Don't leave a single stone unturned,' he told his agents. 'I want this painting, and I don't care what it costs.' He showed them the picture in an art catalogue.

His agents searched high and low and could not quickly

locate the painting. But they eventually returned to Randolph with their report. 'The bad news is that we can't possibly obtain that painting. The good news is that you already have it in your gallery!'

There is nothing—no perversion, no violence, no lie, no deceit—that will not be carried out by man or woman against a fellow human being in the quest of serving King Greed. We have sold out to the lie that while adultery is not OK, greed is OK; worse, that wealth is even a sign of righteousness. Selectively, we skip over the words of St Paul that state directly that greedy people cannot enter the kingdom:

> Neither the sexually immoral nor thieves nor the greedy nor drunkards nor slanderers nor swindlers will inherit the Kingdom of God.
>
> (1 Corinthians 6:10)

Somewhere in America, I'm told, someone is driving around a gold Rolls Royce car with the numberplate GREED on it. And at Harvard Business School, after years of 'anything goes—all's fair in money, love, and war' philosophy, ethics courses have been introduced to respond to the spate of insider trading scandals that have rocked America and other economies. Clever financial wizards who were once eulogised for their inventive wheeling and dealing and creative accounting are only just being seen for what they are: very definitely not OK after all. For Australia, the names of Bond and Skase were once 'you beaut' symbols. Now, they are the symbols of ignominy and anti-social self-interest. I'm not sure the general population is any less greedy—just less successful at it.

Neurosis
One of the many side-effects of greed is an unhealthy self-preoccupation. In a Central American or Filipino base community which is barely surviving against terrorists,

vigilantes, and hypocritical governments, no one sits around bewailing that he doesn't know who he is; no one complains that she's suffering from lack of self-worth because her mother was unkind to her when she was a child. In the West, by contrast, artificial mental break-down is one of the last resorts for people who want to evade the great issues that lie before them. As Woody Allen shows in his film *Manhattan*, when we have every-thing we want materially, when we've tried every sexual position, every country, every food; when we've got so world-weary that there's nothing else left for us, we might as well cultivate some psychological disorders, becoming neurotic to avoid the great questions of the universe. How pitiful that reaction sounds when the poor are always with us. It is significant that Robert Coles (once lauded by a *Time* lead article as 'the greatest psychiatrist in the US') in his Pulitzer Prize winning series 'Children in Crisis' showed that the children of the rich have generally lower self esteem and less moral values framework than the children of the poor.

Isolation

Among those who may have been in the audience when Jesus told his story of the rich fool were at least two men who knew in their hearts the painful clarity of vision Jesus had in that story: Zacchaeus and Matthew. Zacchaeus had been a wealthy chief tax collector, a complete outcast from Jewish culture. For the sake of the almighty shekel he was prepared to be isolated from society. For a start, Zacchaeus would have had to bid for his job, staking personal money against the money of others for the dubious honour of extorting more from the masses. Jewish rabbis of the time—except Jesus—would have regarded him as utterly beyond the pale of God's redeeming love. And then there was Matthew the disciple, who had also been a tax collector. Both these men had been liberated from a false view of God—as one who excludes—because they had encountered him in Jesus as one who loves and includes. They had also been liberated from the greedy compulsion to buy the happiness which they could not find in human relationships.

The first declared signs of Zaccheus' repentance was his promise to give half his belongings to the poor and to return four-fold all he had extorted. There certainly is an economic aspect to repentance, salvation and holiness!

I'll never forget a man who turned up at our house once who was on the run from criminals like himself. He had belonged to what was called the Toe-cutter Gang—men who, when there was a robbery, went after the gang who had made the theft and extorted both information and cash by kidnapping the thieves and then removing their toes one by one with bolt-cutters until they revealed where the stolen money had been hidden.

This man had been on the run for ten years, and there was a contract for $15,000 out on him. He knew that his days were numbered: that it was only a matter of time before one of his money-hungry 'mates' blew the whistle on him and got the $15,000 promised for his capture. So when he arrived on our doorstep he was in stark terror. The soles of his shoes had worn through, as had the soles of his feet, which were raw with infected blisters. Remembering the screams of tortured men, he wept as he told us his story and as he received our small acts of kindness— one of my two pairs of shoes, clean socks, and bandages for his feet. Perhaps he saw for a moment the joy of human loving and giving. At any rate, it was the first time in ten years that he knew community. His departure from this world was permanent, I understand.

When the pain of our relationships with others becomes too intense, we turn to material things for comfort. Like Zacchaeus and Matthew, we are willing to be social outcasts, if we can only surround ourselves with 'good things' and live as we wish. Less and less of our life is given to sharing and caring, and more and more to acquiring and exploiting. Our insurance policies increase; we need alarm bells on our houses and cars; we are weighed down with the onerous task of controlling our portfolios, our bank accounts, our overseas tax shelters...so that the warmth of human contact might as well be something on another planet. Our lives are eaten up with ownership instead of relationship, and only if we commit ourselves to Jesus and his kingdom will greed lose its seductive, addictive stranglehold on us. Only then will we discover instead the joys of serving others. In the story of the rich fool it is noted that in just five verses the terms 'my', 'I', 'himself' or similar ego-isolated words occur at least sixteen times. Greed and lonely individualism go hand in hand.

Greed and the gospel

In 1989 I worked for part of the summer at a camp on radical Christian discipleship. I had just learned that in an Australian survey it was found that, of those who went to church regularly, only 3-4% thought their main reason for being in fellowship with other Christians was to bring healing and help to others. Armed additionally with some other statistics I had learned at the same time from America—that young people there (in a country where 60% go to church) spend altogether $98,000,000,000 on themselves annually—I asked some related questions at the camp.

How much money did the young people (mostly in their 20s) earn after tax each week? How much did they spend on food, board and clothing, how much on entertainment, and how much on bringing the love and help of the gospel to those outside God's kingdom? How much to reduce poverty and suffering? The answer came back loud and clear: an average of no more than 1% of the income each young person earned went to help others in any form. Commitment, apparently, had more to do with enjoying praise worship than with showing love. Yet if even 60% of their collective incomes had been tithed, the sum would have been overwhelmingly helpful to those in need. Just multiply that sum in proportion to the $98 billion spent each year in America, and it's staggering to think what a change the young people of Australia and America (for a start!) could effect on this planet.

We cannot live under the illusion that Christians are immune from the corruption of material greed. While countless individuals lead blameless lives, others band together to twist the good news into bad news. In the late 1980s, for instance, I met up with two Filipino teachers at the World Congress of Evangelisation whose heads were bowed and who had tears in their eyes because of a project they were just embarking on. They had gathered courage after prayer and careful thought to release some information about oppression in the Philippines. Hearing that the literature was about to be released, their supervisors from US based missions who sponsored them told them of the repercussions: 'You release that information,' they said, 'and your institution will lose all its financial support from the West. Not only that, we'll circulate your names and report that you're left-wing extremists.' To do that in the Philippines is virtually to sign a death warrant. How obscene it is that Western Christian prosperity takes upon itself the authority to pervert and enslave the free conscience of indigenous peoples by the manipulation of economic lies and political threats. In spite of the threats, these women released the information and stood up for the truly good news of the gospel—no matter how it reflected on the sponsoring western governments and agencies. They were counting the real cost.

Rich man, poor man

The story of the rich man and Lazarus in Luke's sixteenth chapter is familiar enough, but do we realise just how radical it is? Here's a millionaire who swaggers in and out of his mansion every day making his millions without even seeing the itinerant beggar at his gate. Lazarus, meanwhile, is so ill with leprosy that the local poodles and labradors come and lick his sores. (Can you imagine the scandal if a scene like that were depicted in a modern church's stained glass window? The offence would have been just as great for the pious Jews who heard the story.) Unlike the rich man, Lazarus can't escape his miserable predicament, and he looks with longing at the half-nibbled snacks and delicacies that go out with the bin man every morning, scrambling for the bits that drop. Predictably, he dies of neglect and starvation, unable to help himself, unnoticed and unhelped by the rich man.

The first part of this story makes us realise that we who have the world's plenty go about with our eyes shut—or at least locked into our own selfish pursuits. Unlike Jesus, we don't lower our sights sufficiently to see the underbelly of poverty that is all around us.

In the second part of the story, the roles are reversed. Now Lazarus is in the comforting company of Father Abraham, and it is the rich man who is in the poverty of divine judgement. Looking at Lazarus properly for the first time, the rich man sees a possible solution to his intense pain. 'Send Lazarus just to dip his finger in cool water and drip it on my parched tongue,' he begs.

Seemingly full of regret for his past life, the rich man has not in fact changed his attitude in the least. Just as he built his money on the backs of poor people like Lazarus, so he is still willing to exploit Lazarus, to use him as a messenger boy.

Too often this story (as in the case of its Old Testament counterpart about Sodom and Gomorrah) is interpreted from fundamentalist Christian pulpits as a kind of morality tale with a formula that goes something like this: 'If you're a bad person, you'll burn in hell for ever!' Others interpret the story from the social radical perspective: 'If you don't look after the poor, you'll fry on the other side.' It seems to me that neither of these interpretations is adequate; both groups are making the story suit their own purpose. In fact it is saying something far more radical: that our affluence, greed, self-interest and indifference are robbing us of the ability to respond to God, and therefore of the ability to respond to the suffering Christ in others. Jesus makes that plain, reminding the listeners that it wouldn't make any difference what the Father did, they would still be hard-hearted and unrepentant. 'He said to them, "If they do not listen to Moses and the Prophets, they will not be convinced even if someone rises from the dead" ' (Luke 16:31).

This story makes us ask ourselves some hard questions: do we really want to listen to and obey Jesus? (Or would we just rather go to Christian music and arts festivals and meet with others like ourselves?) Do we really want Christ's kingdom here on earth? (Or are we terrified of the overthrow of the kingdom that is already in our midst and doing us well?)

Can we defend greed?

At the heart of the Christian faith is a dilemma that exposes all believers to difficulties of which they may not even be aware. The Scriptures' teachings are virtually unique among the teachings of most world religions in that they celebrate the material universe. When God saw what he had made, we're told, he said, 'This is good!' So, unlike Greek philosophy, Christianity does not teach a split worldview of matter and spirit being evil and good respectively. Rather, true Christianity celebrates the smell of a rose, the warmth and giving of sexuality, the sound of water cascading down rocks, the sight of trees bursting into leaf. 'The earth is the Lord's, and everything in it, the world, and all who live in it' (Psalm 24:1). True Christianity celebrates and cares for this world, not regarding it with a sense of ownership and prerogative, but with a sense of awed humility, as looking into a reflection of God's wondrous creativity. St Paul assures us God has given us all things that we might enjoy them fully (1 Timothy 6:17).

What, then, has gone wrong? We have twisted that God-given joy in creation to a covetous, consumerist greed that distorts 'use' so that it becomes 'abuse'. Instead of sharing, we hoard. Instead of caring, we kill and destroy—in the name of making money.

Modern Christians cannot claim superior commitment to a celebration of healthy sensuality. Few of us have supported the grassroots green movement—something which should surely have come from the church rather than from the New Age ethos. We're just as busy making money and planning to make money as everyone else, and we have let the obsession permeate our theology as well. Like the Pharisees who looked down on tax collectors such as Zaccheus and Matthew, we may travel to the ends of the earth to make only one convert; we may never miss church or a prayer meeting; we may study the Scriptures and be committed to their inerrancy as God's word; we may cream off the top of our self-indulgent lives the 10% we know belongs to God...but like the Pharisees we also mock Jesus with our greedy consumer culture. Luke 16:13–14 reads, 'When the Pharisees heard this ("You cannot serve God and money") they sneered at Jesus because they loved money.' We are willing to be loved, but we're not willing to be changed.

Orange County, Los Angeles, in the United States Bible belt, is one of the richest suburban regions in the world per capita, but it also has a divorce rate of 78%, even though it is also the prime centre for Spirit-filled churches. What motivates life in Orange County, as for many of us in the West, is not the changing love of Christ, but pure greed. We want everything and, as Freddie Mercury of Queen assured us, we want it now. So we look for ways of justifying our acquisitiveness and come up with the prosperity doctrine: the name-it-claim-it philosophy that touts wealth, not grace; the line of argument that says the best of God's work in the world comes through those who are successful and prosperous.

Paul pours a salutary bucket of cold water on this doctrine. In the same paragraph in which he warns Timothy and his companions about false teachers, he warns about the seductions of material ownership:

> If anyone teaches false doctrines,...he has an unhealthy interest in controversies and arguments that result in constant friction between people of corrupt mind who have been robbed of the truth and who think godliness is a means to financial gain. But godliness with contentment is great gain... *People who want to get rich fall into temptation and a trap and into many foolish and harmful desires that plunge men into ruin and destruction. For the love of money is a root of all kinds of evil.* Some people, eager for money, have wandered from the faith and pierced themselves with many griefs.
>
> (1 Timothy 6:3–10)

Clearly, while enjoyment of God's good gifts to us is healthy, human, and scriptural, we cannot defend greed on any basis—neither health, humanity, nor Scripture.

Greed and the poor

A priest from Central America, Don Helder Camara, summed it all up: 'When I feed the poor, they call me a saint; when I ask why the poor have no food, they call a Communist.' When this saying becomes, 'When I ask why the poor have no food, THEY CALL ME A CHRISTIAN,' I will know we have shown we are serious about the Kingdom of God.

'Blessed are the poor,' said Jesus, echoing the words of his mother Mary. And when the words of Mary's prophetic manifesto for the poor (see Chapter 3) are taken out of the cathedral and onto the streets, they suddenly become fearfully threatening. The book *Unexpected News* by Robert McAfee Brown, tells a moving story that dramatises this truth. In a third-world country under a dominating, autocratic government, it was a special day. All the Catholic Christians were to take part in a parade during which they celebrated and read Mary's Magnificat. So while the poor rejoiced over the words, the wealthy, who also had to read them, reciting them aloud and on show in front of government soldiers who watched, trembled for fear of revolution as they heard the words: 'He has brought down rulers from their thrones but has lifted up the humble. He has filled the hungry with good things and sent the rich empty away' (Luke 1:52).

McAfee Brown states,

> They are singing of a new order, a new world in which all expectations have been turned around. Those in power have their spies and informers inside the meeting, of course, and their army (in the guise of the police) outside the meeting. Surely the police, hearing such revolutionary slogans as 'Put down the mighty from their thrones!' and 'Exalt those of low degree!' should have their guns at the ready as the crowd leaves the assembly hall.
>
> But the crowd understands the wisdom of the serpent as well as the gentleness of the dove. For what can the police, 'good Catholics' all, do? All the worshippers are doing is singing a prayer song by a dutiful, demure little Jewish girl who just happens, as far as those in Lima, Peru, are concerned, to be the Mother of the Lord Jesus Christ.
>
> (*Unexpected News: Reading the Bible with Third World Eyes*, by Robert McAfee Brown, Westminster Press, Philadelphia)

In 1989 at the World Congress on Evangelisation in

Manila, many of the Westerners who attended were wowed by the new convention centre where we met and heard extravagant words of praise for Imelda Marcos, who had encouraged the work on the centre. 'What a creative lady,' I heard people say in hushed tones as we went in.

Having just returned from time among the real Filipinos in the mountains (see Chapter 1), I found the comments nauseating. I seriously doubt it was an appropriate venue for the celebration of the gospel which Jesus said was authenticated by the fact that it was 'preached to the poor' (Luke 11:5). But it was cheaper to have it there, including flights, than in New York!

That convention centre in Manila would not be standing, would not be maintained, without the exploited poor of those islands who painted walls, cemented bricks, and now clean toilets so that the West will be bamboozled into pouring in more aid—not for the suffering poor, however, but for more such needless waste. And this situation is tolerated because investment from the West and the ceiling of the Filipino national debt is determined not by how many poor children are fed and innoculated, not by how many families torn apart by war are united, but by how many grandiose and obscene buildings of that nature can be erected to King Greed.

The hotels of the city are no better. The petite, mini-skirted girls who wait on tables in the hotels are trained to give off that distinctive aroma of Asian 'we-are-here-to-serve-you' charm—one that appeals directly to the libido and greed of the Westerners who are so quickly drawn in by it and who have in fact orchestrated it in the first place. The waitresses, meanwhile, earn little more than 1,000 pesos a month, the price of two New York steaks, for serving huge steaks to Westerners every day. And their seamstress sisters and cousins who can't afford even to feed their children sit in sweatshops and make Parisian gowns on their own sewing machines, gowns that will sell in the so-called developed world for thousands of dollars. Who then can claim that there is no relationship between our greed and their poverty?

Greed for land is as dangerous as for money. North American Indians, Australian Aborigines and many tribes in Africa have no concept of owning land. They know it only as a gift of God to be nurtured, cherished, and renewed after use. Westerners, by contrast, draw boundaries and fight wars, saying, 'This is ours, we will use it as we wish. If we own it, we're within our rights to exploit it in any way. And even if we don't use it and it lies empty, it is still ours because we've paid for it.'

The theory runs like this: ownership can be achieved by payment and entitles us to exploit the land. Such an argument destroyed millions of Indians in North America, and countless Aborigines in Australia—for political expedience and greed, not for any arguments of Christian justice ('I've tilled this land so it's mine, and the savages can't use it or take it away from me now. God gave us this land!') Such an argument leaves dolphins thrashing in fishing nets, whales bleeding on decks, and strip-mine deserts where once there was arable soil. Such an argument sends Bangladeshi grain on cargo ships to fatten cows and hogs for American steaks and hams. Such an argument strips South America of rain forests, precious medicinal herbs, and fragile indigenous cultures. Such an argument fells Australian trees, few as they are, for the Japanese wood-chipping industry. Such an argument rolls tanks and bulldozers into houses built for the poor in the Philippines. Such an argument leaves land, animals, and people subjected to indignity and rape. Such an argument defaces the image of God in all creation.

Freedom from greed: God's grace

All of us are prone to greed, an uncomfortable truth which the Apostle James addressed in his epistle:

> You want something but don't get it. You kill and covet, but you cannot have what you want. You quarrel and fight. You do not have because you do not ask God…Anyone who becomes a friend of the world becomes an enemy of God. Or do you think Scripture says without reason that the spirit he caused to live in us envies intensely? But he gives us more grace.
>
> (James 4:2, 4–6).

Does our guilty involvement in the world's greed mean we are called to an ascetic lifestyle that can enjoy none of the gifts God has given us? No, it means that we are to give in to grace, placing our hope in God's boundless generosity and being generous in turn to the needy around us. Grace, not harsh asceticism, is the opposite of greed.

Grace is, by definition, freely given. Yet both materially and spiritually, Christians act as if we had to earn our way in—either to the earthly club, or to the heavenly 'club'. We have shortened the list of sins to a list of private sins. We have then shortened that list further to an even smaller one, one that leaves out greed—the very sin Jesus had the harshest words for—because it leads to so much other sin. In so doing we have left the poor—both materially and spiritually speaking—outside in the cold. In so doing we have abandoned the Old and New Testament teaching and instead aligned 'wickedness' more often with trivial legalism than with greed for material and spiritual prosperity at others' expense.

> I hate, I despise your religious feasts;
> I cannot stand your assemblies.
> Even though you bring me burnt offerings and grain offerings,
>   I will not accept them…

> Away with the noise of your songs!
> > I will not listen to the music of your harps.
> But let justice roll on like a river
> > righteousness like a never-failing stream.
>
> (Amos 5:21–24)

We cannot afford to confuse churchiness with right-eousness—which has to do with justice, not Christian meetings!

God wants us to speak for the poor whose voice is too faint to be heard. He is asking us to understand the tragedies around us and to be heart-wounded about them. Middle-class housewives and corporate executives wouldn't need Valium to get to sleep if they worked for the poor in 'boring' moments when 'there's nothing else to do':

> Speak up for those who cannot speak for themselves,
> > for the rights of all who are destitute.
> Speak up and judge fairly;
> > defend the rights of the poor and needy.
>
> (Proverbs 31:8–9)

When Jesus, his insides knotted up with anguish and compassion (Matthew 9:36ff), looked at the poor, then at the Pharisees, he attacked the Pharisees not for preaching in unorthodox ways, but for their hypocrisy in manipulating laws so that widows were extorted and their homes repossessed (Mark 12:40; Matthew 23:14; Luke 20:47). St Paul aligned himself with that kind of compassion—as well as that kind of denunciation—when he wrote to the Romans about the real meaning of the kingdom of God:

> The kingdom of God is of righteousness (ie, justice), peace and joy in the Holy Spirit, because anyone who serves Christ in this way is pleasing to God and approved by men.
>
> (Romans 14:17–18)

There's nothing cheap or easy about this kind of kingdom, for Paul is not writing about a half-asleep comfort zone where everyone is holy, happy, and at ease with himself; he is not writing about cheap tears shed over starving babies in the Horn of Africa and shown on video clips that do more to exalt the promoters than the poor— me first, me second, and me last. No, the word we have translated as 'righteousness' in fact means 'justice and peace' in its original Hebrew, Aramaic and Greek forms: the sort of spiritual and physical wholeness we call peace affects social, emotional, relational, political and spiritual life—*shalom*, not just the cessation of conflict. And within that kingdom of God, mercy and grace flow through everything—art, love, politics, families. Anything less is not the kingdom; it's the cosy comfort zone again:

> The Spirit of the Lord is upon me,
>   because he has anointed me
>   to preach good news to the poor.
> He has sent me to proclaim freedom for the prisoners
>   and recovery of sight for the blind,
>   to release the oppressed.

(Luke 4:18)

The world has yet to see in our lifetime a major movement in the church that will identify unapologetically and consistently with the poor and the oppressed, as Jesus did. And until that happens, the church does not mirror the image of Jesus in the New Testament. This view isn't something for liberation theologians in Central America; it's something for Christians in Brixton and Toxteth, Melbourne and Sydney, New York and Atlanta and Los Angeles.

6

Sexuality, Sense and Shalom

If ever there was a need for reconciliation between peoples, it is now. In Chapter 7 we'll be looking at the need for reconciliation between those of different races, but there is an even more ancient need for reconciliation today: between men and women. The problems between men and women are neither solely of men's making, nor of women's. Nor is the love-hate tension between us simply a matter of human wickedness or oppression.

Men can no longer relate to women as they did in the past, defending their actions by attacking women's 'bloody-mindedness' or 'weakness'; and women can no longer keep their strength, courage and wisdom under wraps out of a false or co-dependent fear of threatening men. Relationships between men and women require the same depth of healing — reconciliation, patience, forgiveness and simple conversation — as the relationships between races and nations. We can't expect too much too fast, but when issues of human sexuality and gender are looked at honestly in the light of God's love and grace, things can and do change. We can discover the true basis for our sexuality, for our creativity, for our identity — since all these things are tied together.

There is one major difference between human beings and animals, but it is not in the arena of needing to express our sexuality. Dogs do it, grasshoppers do it, kangaroos do it, parrots do it, lions do it, snails do it, whales do it, and so do human beings. Nothing unusual! But I often talk to young men who sincerely believe that their entire identity depends on their sexual prowess. That idea makes me laugh *and* makes me sad, because it brings back a memory or two...

I once worked as a jackaroo in Western Queensland. Like an American cowboy I was on horseback all day mustering the animals, but they were sheep, not cattle. I learned quickly that if a ram slips into a paddock of a hundred ewes for just one night, he can put to shame the most red-blooded of men. Even a weak ram makes a man look pitiful—there won't be many ewes not in lamb by the next morning! No, the difference between human beings and animals lies in the human capacity to ask questions about the universe. 'Why am I here? Where do I belong?' And when we don't get satisfactory answers, we know we are in pain...and can reflect on that, too. When gender/sexuality are divorced from intelligence, relationship, spirituality and a tribal-social sense of responsibility, disaster is round the corner.

We certainly need now to reflect on where we are as sexual beings. God has given us the ability to say 'yes' or 'no' to things. Though we have sexual appetites as animals do, we aren't driven by the same pure instinct that drives animals. As human beings we are quite capable of distinguishing love from lust. It's a nonsense when a young man says to his girl, 'This is causing me pain, so if you love me, you'll let me'; for if she tells him to wait and he walks off, then she never had a lover, only a user. It's therefore up to each of us to look our own sexuality in the face, neither running from it nor submerging ourselves in it as if it alone defined our being. Hundreds of years ago Descartes postulated 'I think, therefore I am.' In these obsessive days we have rewritten this thesis to say 'I copulate, therefore I am.' The consequence is massive sexual neurosis, relationless intimacy and sexual violence.

Sobering statistics

By the year 2000, according to a recent study done by a family policy study centre in London, at least 50% of all children will be living outside what we call an historic normal family structure. The mythical happy family of mum, dad, and 1.8 or 2.4 kids (according to country) hardly exists now and will be even more rare a decade from now. Many marriages in the West last only five or six years, partly because we enter marriage with such desperation and with so many illusions that the relationship hardly stands a chance in the first place.

As I have already mentioned, the heart of the USA West Coast Bible Belt, in Orange County, California has a divorce rate of 78%. Christians there fare little better than anyone else, many having been in three marriages. 'Civilisation as we know it' is breaking down, and the youngsters growing up in those homes—Christian or not—have had their lives confused and shattered by it all.

Surveys conducted in Australia in recent years have suggested that many men believed that it was acceptable for a man to beat his wife in certain situations including if she didn't have sex with him when he wanted it. Sexual abuse of children is rife, clearly involving the well educated—some of them are even the pastors of churches, men who do not live on the frightening edge of life by any stretch of the imagination. They aren't 'over there, somewhere'; they're right here among us.

Given this terrifying situation representing an even more terrifying attitude, perhaps it's no wonder that in Australia, at least, 65% of all marriages end at the instigation of the women; 19% by mutual agreement; and only 16% by the decision of the men. Women have decided that they can't take any more of the pain and (in some cases) enslavement. Ladies and gentlemen, we do have a problem! The more long-term frightening reality is that as we are essentially tribal animals, the freedoms introduced by the Enlightenment have spawned rampant individualism, rather than strengthening tribal roots and family.

Great expectations

When you marry the one you love, you begin with the illusion that you're entering at least twenty years of bliss. It isn't long before the bliss wears off and the blisters set in, as everyone discovers. The gap between the dream world and reality suddenly yawns before us, and we fall into it, burning out because of our illusions.

An excellent book to read about the crises facing Western civilisation is *Wild Hope* by Tom Sine (Monarch Publications, 1992). A few quotes illustrating the incredible environment in which we attempt to foster relationships are given below:

> A Washington Post/ABC News Poll found that Baby Boomers (born 1946-64) were twice as likely as those of the previous generation to approve of men and women living together without the benefit of marriage. In other words, the criteria for social conduct shifted for the Boomers from accepted social norms to 'what's best for me in my life now'.

> Never has a generation believed so strongly that their first duty is to themselves.

> Americans from the very first have tended to value autonomy and individualism over community and tradition.

> …'expressive individualism' has already altered American morality, religion, and politics…. Because of this ethic, Baby Boomers are less likely to sacrifice themselves for family, friends, or society than the Booster generation (ie, born 1927-45).

Many Boomers, when making decisions about marriage and family, have made those decisions according to 'what's best for me'.

Demographers predict that while nine of every ten Baby Boomers will marry at least once, one in five will divorce twice. And the children of these divorces will rarely see their biological fathers. Fully one third of the children of Boomers will live with step-parents, in 'blended families', with their own particular set of challenges.

In the American magazine *New Dimensions*, Roy Masters finds a direct link between the disintegration of the family and the rise in street gangs.

Most gang members are male. They're usually in their teens to mid-20's. They come from disadvantaged socio-economic backgrounds, but there is one particular trait many have in common that predisposes them to being drawn into a gang family—the absence of a positive male role model in their own families. Over the many years, many feminists have maintained that the male role model is not altogether necessary in raising male children. However, faced with the shocking results of 20 years of liberation from traditional ideals of the male role model, experts and feminists alike in the USA are now coming round to a stark realisation. Young men without fathers are not going to draw a male identity from their mothers, but rather will seek out a strong male influence they can emulate. One that embodies the masculine side of the family unit.

To put it bluntly, they are looking for a father substitute, but the type of father they are going to get on the streets is a shadowy reflection of the loving, patient protector a father ought to be. Unfortunately, these father-family substitutes are available in ample supply in the ghettos. They provide protection, security, a sense of belonging and a warped male identity to the insecure and already traumatised fatherless ghetto youth. They are known as gangs.

I find myself asking whether we have too quickly forgotten the lessons that any basic tribe in human history could teach us. Substantial evidence suggests that the breakdown of marriage, while freeing hundreds of thousands of couples from what many regarded often as an intolerable situation for them as partners, is often for the children, an unmitigating psychological and social disaster. The consequences of this for our nations, in the end, could be absolutely catastrophic—not just with respect to our interpersonal relationships, but with respect to the whole understanding of the meaning and purpose of life. There is an innate desire for a tribal sense of community, something that goes beyond even just mum and dad, to a wider sense of belonging.

Martin Luther King said:

> An individual has not started living until he (or she) rises above the narrow confines of his (or her) own individualistic concerns, to the broader concerns of ALL humanity. Every man (or woman) must decide whether they will walk in the light of creative altruism or in the darkness of destructive selfishness. This is the judgment—life's most persistent and urgent question is, 'What are we doing for others?'

The church is as full of false teaching about relationships between men and women as are television, advertising, and videos. The lie is abroad that if we have committed our lives to Jesus it automatically follows that all our relationships will be perfect. Sometimes, in fact, the very reverse is true: that some people are so uptight in their expression of faith that they ruin their marriages without really trying!

Both Christians and non-Christians enter marriage these days with high hopes. Men expect too much sexually from their mates, and often too much domestically. Women expect too much romantically, lulling themselves with adolescent views of roses, milk and honey all the way. But no one is as bad as his or her worst moments, and no one is as good as his or her best moments. When we're married, we get all those moments, bad and good. It's possible, then, for a woman to wear her man down with niggling and nagging over small things, and forget all the loving and good things he does. It's equally possible for a man to wear his wife down with day after day of insensitive, demanding, and even brutish or violent behaviour, overlooking the loving and sacrificial things she does. It's at this point that people who have been sailing on the sea of make-believe crash onto the rocks of reality.

If we are dedicated to the ideal of romantic love as the basis for marriage, our love and our marriage will be in danger, and we are candidates for burn-out.

In the *Los Angeles Times*, journalist Mary Jo Kochakian reported the opinions of psychologist Alaya M. Pines in an article entitled 'Marry, but don't expect too much.' Ms Pines, author of the book *Keeping the Spark Alive* (published in the United States by Martin's Press), stated:

> If you want life to be lived on a dream cloud of love, constant intimacy and magic, and if you expect the simple act of marriage to find focus and meaning in your life, to answer all of life's basic questions, you are going to be disappointed. Hang on to those notions and you guarantee burn-out in your relationship.

Ms Pines is only too right. Christian parents want their kids to be 'nice'. They want them to speak politely, say thank-you at the appropriate times, read the Bible, and marry some other nice Christian young person when the time comes—preferably after becoming successful executives who can provide comfortably for their wives and children. We are caught in the same dangerous psycho-sexual-romantic trap as everyone else, and we need to confront it!

Before becoming my full-time researcher, my friend Trevor Chambers gave time to some modern prophesying, dressing himself up in various simple disguises and carrying placards up and down the central shopping mall of Melbourne—a city of three million people. At that time a computer programmer for the public service, he attracted a lot of media attention for wearing the head gear—an inverted bucket with a hole for the eyes—of Australia's most famous historic bush ranger (outlaw) Ned Kelly. This was well accentuated by his 6'3" (190 cm) height and his Rasputin-like (and Ned-Kelly-like) long dark beard. His placards associated modern day accountants, lawyers and business people with the outlaw image—whereas Ned Kelly robbed banks with guns, the modern day elite used guile and the letter of the law to avoid taxes and thereby steal from the public purse.

Tackling the issue of relationships, he donned a full long bridal veil, complete with a head piece of cheap pink plastic flowers and carried a double-sided placard announcing 'Don't Try to get from Marriage what you can only get from God' and 'Sex is not a Cure for Emptiness.' Trevor's ability to be able to make fun of himself enabled people to open up.

'You're right,' some men said to him. 'She hasn't delivered what I wanted at all.' 'You're right,' said some women. 'I thought my man could be everything to me, but life just doesn't work out that way.'

Trev was making an important point. When we try to get from another human being what we can only find in God, when we are longing for full satisfaction from another person, we will end up ship-wrecked. The relationship will be under the pressure of impossible expectations; no other person can ever meet all our needs. Our partners will feel guilty that they can't, and we will feel angry that they can't. Mick Jagger's song 'I can't get no satisfaction' speaks for anyone who tries to find total fulfilment in sexual expression. In the end, without the meaning and mission Jesus supplies, there is no ultimate satisfaction in any relationship.

Sex and worship

Tabloids trumpeting titles that mix a heady combination of sex and religion generally attract a good readership. There's something that appeals to the voyeur in all of us when an Irish bishop or an American televangelist is caught behaving like any other human being (surprise, surprise!). We know instinctively that sex and religion are interconnected; that those who abandon themselves to the ecstasies of religion are equally capable of abandoning themselves to the ecstasies of sex. So, either openly or quietly, we rub our hands in glee at the juicy scuttlebutt.

Why? Perhaps it's because, whether we're conscious of the fact or not, we're all made to worship. We may think we're driven by sex and greed, but in the end these are only analgesics against the pain of the failure to fulfill our deepest need of all, one which must be satisfied somehow: to love and worship. We may not even acknowledge God in our lives, but it is he who has made us sexual beings, and he who has created us to worship. When we don't worship and adore God, therefore, we turn our worship to other human beings, searching for the kind of perfection, joy and fulfilment we would have found in God if we had been willing to make the commitment and express our faith. We rush, then, from real worship to idolatry. When we feel that erotic, emotional rush, we persuade ourselves that we're in reality, that we're discovering our identity. We have instead bought into the Greek mythological concept of love, in which Eros's arrows have pierced and blinded us and there's no escape. Of course that kind of romantic love will never stand the test of time. It is not insignificant that the traditional Cupid is blindfolded.

Love (sexual, romantic love) is blind and needs the guidance of mind, the Spirit and the wisdom of the tribe to make wise choices.

It's psycho-sexual romanticism that starts such relationships, and according to a number of studies, that kind of romance has little chance of lasting more than three to six months. I remember vividly one man who bounded into my house early in the week with a whoop of joy and a huge smile on his face. 'I want a wedding on Friday!' he demanded. I told him to cool it; in Australia the law requires notice of at least a month and a day. Then I spent the next month quizzing him and trying to talk him out of it; he had met the girl only three days before and scarcely knew her. 'I was at a party,' he told me. 'She came in one door, and I came in the other. That was it.'

I couldn't convince them to wait, and the marriage lasted exactly a week and a half. Their decision had been based on adrenalin, not on mature, committed love; their decision had been based on idolatry, not on real worship, intelligent choice, or self-giving humility. *While we read and study for perhaps seven or eight years for a career, we may not give even as many as seven or eight days to a proper study of the practical and emotional differences between men and women, the way sex works, or the essential nature of real communication and commitment.* We have learned nothing about resolving conflict, except the destructive patterns our parents have taught.

Rushing into erotic idolatry is one false path we can follow. Another equally false path is to turn moralist and sit in judgement on current sexual mores, as if we were somehow above it all. When we follow that path, we are missing the point. Sexual licence isn't just an outward sign of the inner awfulness of human nature, the unredeemed passions of the 'old man'. Sexual licence is rather in part an outward sign of the inner hunger for God and for intimacy with a Being who will not fail us in any way. It's no use then to point the finger; we should rather be weeping for the breakdown of ideals that inevitably accompanies the shattering of illusions. We should rather be ministering to people in their brokenness and hunger, not with judgementalism, but with the grace that Jesus gives.

Our rock songs howl 'I need you' (to fill the personal, social and cosmic emptiness in my life) with tragic and predictable desperation. Just consider the following lyrics from popular songs:

BAD ENGLISH sing:

> When I see your smile, I can face the world
> You know I can do anything.
>
> (Copyright: Sony)

Michael Bolton adds:

> How am I supposed to live without you...
> When all that I've been living for is gone?
>
> (Copyright: Sony)

and Linda Ronstadt's song 'I Don't Know Much' says:

> So many questions still left unanswered
> So much I've never broken through
> And when I feel you near me sometimes I see so clearly
> The only truth I've ever known is me and you.
>
> (Copyright: WEA)

In the true sense, the words 'I love you' rarely enter in.

We start relationships because we are hungry for the kind of intimacy that only God can give, and we thus confuse intimacy with sexuality. Christians and non-Christians alike make this mistake, grabbing for romance because it seems like the last magic potion in a dying and broken world, a final shoring against the tide of pain that threatens to engulf us. We lose ourselves in the Elvis

Presley escapist paradise either because we don't know God, or because we do but can't face the pain he wants to help us walk through. We idolise human relationships and worship at their shrine because we haven't been able to satisfy our desire for real worship. We turn our longings outward, looking for our identity in someone else, looking desperately for the adoring love we haven't directed at the one who really deserves it: God himself.

The woman at the well

> When a Samaritan woman came to draw water, Jesus said to her, 'Will you give me a drink?'...The Samaritan woman said to him, 'You are a Jew and I am a Samaritan woman. How can you ask me for a drink?' (For Jews do not associate with Samaritans.)...Jesus answered her, 'Everyone who drinks this water will be thirsty again, but whoever drinks the water I give will never thirst. Indeed, the water I give will become in him a spring of water welling up to eternal life.' The woman said to him, 'Sir, give me this water so that I won't get thirsty and have to keep coming here to draw water.' He told her, 'Go and call your husband and come back.' 'I have no husband,' she replied...Jesus said to her '...The fact is, you have had five husbands, and the man you now have is not your husband. What you have just said is quite true.' 'Sir,' the woman said, 'I can see you are a prophet. Our fathers worshipped on this mountain, but you Jews claim that the place where we must worship is in Jerusalem.' Jesus declared, 'Believe me, woman, a time is coming when you will worship the Father neither on this mountain nor in Jerusalem. You Samaritans worship what you do not know; we worship what we do know, for salvation is from the Jews. Yet a time is coming and has now come when the true worshippers will worship the Father in spirit and truth.
>
> (John 4:7–24)

Many people today would identify with the woman at

the well. They might not have had five husbands, but they have probably been in and out of more than five relationships, and they are still longing for intimacy and fulfilment. When the woman admitted that she had no husband, she was in fact saying more than we who read this passage in English realise; the words for 'husband' and 'object of worship' in Aramaic are from the same root; so when Jesus tells her prophetically that she had no husband, he's speaking not only on the literal level but also putting his finger on the heart of her need: she has no one to worship and adore.

This is precisely how Jesus would like to deal with us. When we are sinning, when we are failing in our sexuality, when our self-image dwindles and we are driven into cheap gratification to satisfy ourselves—it's precisely then that he draws close to us as he did to the woman at the well. 'I love you,' he says, 'and I understand how small you feel. I am closer to you than you know. I gave my life to free you from your pain. Go on, yell at me all you want and get it off your chest. But when you've finished, if you listen carefully, you'll hear me telling you again, "I love you." When you give your love to me, all other loves will pale into insignificance, and you will be satisfied with the water of life that never runs out or dries up.'

I ache when I reread this story of the woman at the well. I ache because the church rarely meets in this loving way people who are derailed by their sexual needs. The church may be the last place, in fact, that they turn to for help. They would rather join Sexaholics Anonymous or Sexual Addicts anonymous. Yet if the church responded more like Jesus, people would come flocking, for the Scriptures (specifically the words of Jesus and John the Baptist) say clearly that tax collectors and prostitutes are going into heaven ahead of theologians and pew-warmers. How tragic that our self-righteousness means that we can't take these words seriously.

Worship defaced: twisted sexuality

Sex as greed

At its most extreme, sex is a form of rampant consumerism built on the attitude that if we can afford it, if it is 'ours' for the taking, we can have it however we like it.

I once spoke to a large group of headmasters and teachers from Australian Christian schools. Many of them were from Pentecostal, Brethren, and Baptist backgrounds, and all were conservative in outlook, committed to the inerrancy of Scripture. They knew of my attitudes towards sex and marriage and, perhaps thinking there was nothing too radical I could say, invited me to speak to them on a pro-family theme. I'm afraid I upset the applecart with my first words, 'Which of you believes in human slavery?'

Not a hand went up. I asked again, and silence still reigned. I went on to describe scenes of slavery in the Deep South in graphic terms: the indignity that white slave owners inflicted on young women (especially), making them stand naked before prospective buyers, fingering them, showing off their breasts and the width of their pelvises to draw attention to the women's capacity to birth more slaves for greedy plantation owners.

I'm sure the men thought as I talked that I'd fallen out of my gumtree altogether this time. I could hear the whispers around the hall, 'Well, what's all this got to do with family?'

I looked them in the eye. 'Are you Bible-believing?' They all nodded enthusiastically. 'Then what have you done to that verse which says that slaves must obey their masters?' I asked. They stared back at me uneasily. 'And if you can ignore that verse because in today's context slavery is an obscenity, how come you can't ignore the verses in St Paul's writings that you feel permit you to dish out ill-treatment to your womenfolk?'

I had no sense of triumph or smugness as I asked these questions: my wife Glena and I have been through enough heartaches of our own because of the learning I'm still doing in my attitudes towards her. But I knew I was in for furious antagonism, and I got it. Those men couldn't face their own inconsistency.

Another thing those men couldn't have faced—and which the church as a whole would much prefer to pretend is not happening—is incest. Again, it's not just something 'out there' among those who don't know God. It's something among us—something to which we need to respond and speak against when we see it.

One night, after hearing some disturbing information about the behaviour of some of the radical youth in my church, I gave a rather conservative address on sexual morality. I received a long letter from one of the young women in the congregation. In angry, hurting words she wrote several pages that shook me for weeks afterwards:

> You told me tonight that I should keep my body for someone who would love me and care for me. Well, my _____ father made that decision for me when I was seven years of age, and he did it right the way through until I was sixteen or seventeen years of age...

Since then I've heard many more such tales, some of them from Christian young people. One girl I remember vividly broke down crying while I was addressing a group of about one thousand high school kids. As I counselled her afterwards I learned that she had a lesbian mother who had more or less abandoned her to the sick fantasies of her father, uncle, grandfather and brother, who had abused and gang-raped her repeatedly for years until she had no concept left of the meaning of love—and certainly no inkling of the meaning of a loving Divine Parent. We can run away from this sort of raw pain and horror by covering our eyes, ears, and mouths, but we won't then be the salt and light in society that Christ commands us to be.

The will to have power over others and over the earth's resources is at the back of any action that manipulates the world and its relationships for personal gratification. Viktor Frankl—Founder of the 3rd Viennese School of Psychotherapy (Following Freud's and Adler's Schools) and author of the best-seller *Man's Search for Meaning*—described the situation with painful clarity. When we have a society, he says, which lacks a central meaning to its existence (he wasn't referring to ecstatic religious experience but to an intelligent, deep sense that life is significant and meaningful) then the psychological consequences for that society are rampant libido (sexual desire) and the 'will to power' (in a capitalist society that means rampant greed). A society without real faith and meaning is a society locked into greed in all its horrific forms—including the coveting of one's neighbour's spouse!!

Sex as analgesic

'I wanna feel the heat with somebody' sang Whitney Houston a few years ago. And we have bought into the lie that sex can transport us out of pain into a magic kingdom. Sex has become a drug.

Analgesics take many forms besides the obvious white pills in a bottle to fend off a headache. They appear also as workaholism, entertainment, fantasy, the shop-till-you-drop syndrome, rock music, devotion to intense exercise, television, video...you name it. The cheapest analgesics for many however, especially young people, is probably sex. Perhaps the parents' marriage is breaking apart, or perhaps the parents are repressive, so the quick fix for a better sense of self-worth is a roll in the nearest field with the girlfriend or boyfriend. The trouble is that after that fix, there has to be another...and another...until (if ever) we do discover real meaning and self-worth in God. Of the thousands of acts of sex on television every year, statisticians tell us that only 2% occur within marriage. We believe the fantasy that sex outside a steady, committed relationship is somehow more exciting—and certainly the ultimate therapy when searching for self esteem. As with chemical addiction—after the rush (or orgasm) the 'hanging out' becomes a slavery and the syndrome does anything BUT build healthy self worth. The Medical Journal of Australia ran a lead article a few years ago on the proposition that sex is *the* drug for our culture.

Sex as mechanics

Pornography has a lot to answer for. Again, though, we're not just talking about human wickedness but about a society driven to desperation and sickness by the longing for worship and fulfilment. In Australia, for example, it's the very city where the Federal Parliament sits that has free rein to mail pornographic literature all over the nation. We turn a blind eye to porn, yet if animal rights activists showed the same concern for women and children who are abused on X-rated videos for the titillation of the perverse, as they do for animals suffering research operations, porn shops and blue movie factories would be closed down within twenty-four hours.

So why do we tolerate pornography—particularly of the violent and incestuous kind? One reason is that in our shallow thinking the depiction of 'relationships' between men and women (though that is hardly the right word) is all right in any form, especially if it helps some marriages 'improve'. We have thus taken away our spontaneity and given ourselves mechanistic sex.

I must admit the silence concerning the link between violence and sex worries me far more than the softer variety of erotica—yet very little is said by thinking Christians concerning the violence issue.

By failing to place our sexuality under the kind of

examination that brings us to mature, intelligent decision-making, we have not only lowered ourselves to the level of dogs in the street, but we are actually beginning to destroy our own sexual capacity. More men than ever are impotent now. Many cannot become aroused unless there is a blue video showing in the bedroom. What could and should be a loving choice becomes instead a biochemical urge to which we give ourselves regardless of the emotional and physical consequences. We have mechanised sex, become anxious about it and so destroyed it for ourselves.

British poet Steve Turner says it so well in this poem:

> Tonight, we will
> fake love together.
> You my love, possess
> all the essential qualities
> as listed by *Playboy*.
> You will last me for
> as long as two weeks
> or until such a time
> as your face and figure
> go out of fashion.
> I will hold you close
> to my Hollywood-standard body
> ...
> I will prop my paperback
> Kama Sutra
> on the dressing table
> and like programmed souls
> we will perform
> ...
> Tonight we will be both
> quick and silent, our time limited,
> measured out in distances
> between fingers
>   and pushbuttons.
>   (UP TO DATE by Steve Turner [Hodder and Stoughton])

We have reduced human tenderness and compassion (in the full sense of that word) to a dehumanised mechanical process. We can't possibly call what goes on in the back of a car on Friday and Saturday nights between two teenagers 'making love'. It's not. There's no other word for it but 'screwing around'—a phrase that raises hackles among Christians but is the only one apt for the situation; it's rude and crude, as is the behaviour it describes.

The end result of mechanised sex is disillusionment. Of course, as Christians we are appalled by anything so extreme and destructive as porn, but we don't seem to see our own inconsistencies and tackle our own failing relationships. We make little effort to change our relationships, and our sex within marriage may be even more sterile and unloving than sex between two people who acknowledge God not at all. We are plastic.

Sex as loneliness

Loneliness often masquerades as sex. Picture the scene, and we've all been there. A teenage boy is alone in his room, hungry for loving, for intimacy. Maybe he's just come back from a youth camp where he's dedicated his life to God. But now he's alone again at home in a hostile environment with no more charismatic choruses, no more warm fuzzies. He feels guilty, but he starts touching himself for comfort... For a second, with the rush of orgasm, he has a sense of 'I-amness', but then it's gone and the loneliness hits him worse than ever—because added to the loneliness is guilt and further isolation.

Is he a wicked pervert, as some preachers would have us believe? Or is he just a lonely kid who hasn't met and discovered the fulfilment of mature, committed, giving love? Again, we can sit in judgement (somehow forgetting we've been there ourselves!) Or we can see through the masturbation to the loneliness. We can write him off, or, as Jesus would, we can tell him that in God's Kingdom there are no more tears, no more loneliness. We can hug him, welcome him into fellowship as a fellow human being and fellow believer and help him grow up into mature sexuality. There is a need for much conversation concerning the religious conflicts over masturbation but this is not the book to deal with this in detail. Suffice it to say— certainly obsessive masturbation is viewed even by most secular therapists as pathological evidence of emotional needs.

Sex and shalom

Knowing that at the back of human sexual expression is a deep longing for intimacy and acceptance helps us understand the way we function as sexual beings. Women have less difficulty in this regard than do men. Whereas research now shows that men actually suffer prolonged physical and mental stress from marital conflict, women often face it more courageously and with less damage because they see it as a pathway to greater intimacy. The fact that the wife may break down in tears before her man substantiates the sad myth that it is women who can't cope; in reality, it is their menfolk who are emotionally so blocked that they no longer know how they feel about anything and can't express their feelings. Whereas women come through marital upheavals feeling stronger, more independent, and pleased with having taken responsibility for clearing the air, men frequently feel weak and helpless in the face of what they often term women's irrational behaviour. 'She's so emotional when I try to analyse the problems,' the man moans. 'He will never commit himself to personal feelings—if I can get him to talk to me at all,' the woman answers. 'And to make matters worse, he puts me down for expressing my own feelings.'

We need to get rid of the old stereotype of hysterical woman meeting rational, logical man if we are to move forward in our emotional and sexual relationships. Men need to wake up to real intimacy—not to fake it. The gospel of Christ is about vulnerability and love, not about power games and put-downs. The more vulnerable we become, the further we move from power and control; the more vulnerable we become, the nearer we move to self-surrender (not mere self-control) and to real love. We have only to look at Jesus to see this: to see his relaxed dealings with prostitutes and with all women. Several excellent books on the 'male intimacy' question are now available—*Male Intimacy; The McGill Report* by McGill (Harper and Row); *The Hazards of Being Male* by Herb Goldberg (Signet); *Healing the Soul* by Gordon Dalbey (Word).

Where then can we find sexual shalom—the wholeness of true love-making? There are at least four places to begin: humility, thoughtfulness, commitment and communication. Four old-fashioned words, perhaps, but all of them reflect mature sexuality; all of them reflect a Christian response to others.

Humility

If there's any blessing in the breakdown of marriage and belief in marriage in Western culture, it's that for the first time (both within and without the church) men can no longer hide in the skirts of a distorted understanding of headship in relationships. Men have abused the privilege of leadership and abused their women mentally, if not physically, sometimes even justifying their behaviour on a manipulated application of biblical principle. Such tragic patterns of behaviour are ending as women take courage to speak and act against them. And within the church these changes give both men and women the opportunity to exercise a far more fundamental biblical principle: that of servanthood and tender compassion. We have only to read the Book of Isaiah or Paul's letter to the Philippians to understand the challenge:

> Surely he took up our infirmities
>   and carried our sorrows,
> yet we considered him stricken by God,
>   smitten by him, and afflicted.
> But he was pierced for our transgressions,
>   he was crushed for our iniquities...
> And by his wounds we are healed.
>
> (Isaiah 53:4–5)

> If you have any encouragement from being united with
> Christ, if any comfort from his love, if any fellowship with
> the Spirit, if any tenderness and compassion, then make
> my joy complete by being like-minded, having the same
> love...in humility consider others better than your-
> selves.... Your attitude should be the same as that of
> Christ Jesus: Who being in the very nature of God, did not
> consider equality with God something to be grasped, but
> made himself nothing, taking the very nature of a ser-
> vant...he humbled himself and became obedient to
> death—even death on a cross!
>
> (Philippians 2:1–8)

If Jesus himself can surrender his life to and for others,
and if we claim to love and serve him, how can we do less?

Thoughtfulness

Deep down we know that the seat of everything creative in
us is somehow placed by the miracle of God's creation not
between our legs but between our ears. Even the most
important sex organ is between our ears! It's there that
compassion, sensuality, tenderness, excitement, and creative loving all arise. Why is it, then, that we can't take
our Christian discipleship as seriously in matters of intelligent sexuality as we can when it comes to sending men
and women into space or developing miracle medicines for
the sick and dying? Why is it that we can apply our minds
to science without apology, but when it comes to faith's
relevance to human relationships we shut off our minds

and stop living sensibly? Instead we stomach the erotic nonsense that pours from screens and books, and we stop thinking. It's not safe sex we need but intelligent, responsible and relational sex!

It's not that we need to go on some sort of head trip that denies the essential importance of feelings—that should be obvious from other things we've considered in this chapter—but that we need to think seriously about relationships not only as we enter them but as they unfold into maturity. To get married, to be linked with someone else for a lifetime—that's an awesome choice: one that demands godly intelligence and a determination to understand what kind of creature we are going to be living with. The God who created human beings, male and female, is the same God who wants to offer us his discernment and wisdom to understand everything from male and female hormones to gentleness and strength as *both* expressed by *both* women and men.

It's often said that the grass is greener on the other side of the fence. In fact, as Dr Joyce Burrows has said, it's the grass that gets the most water that is the greenest, no matter which side of the fence it's on. Marriages burn out when expectations are unreal, or when there's a lack of deep thinking about the meaning of what we do in them. So marriages that are to remain alive need to be fostered with loving thoughtfulness and intelligence. Our marriages cannot afford to be isolated from our world view, our service of humanity, our long term vocation or calling in life. Choose carefully, live wisely.

Commitment

We've seen that the good life isn't just about warm fuzzies: it's about truth in relationships, about commitment. When the three-month excitement of psycho-sexual love wears off, we have to work at our relationships and we have to want to work at them, including re-creating romantic love. It's no use mistaking hormonal drives for the will of God.

Like the different kinds of soil in Jesus' story of the sower, we are all made with hearts that can become stony, weed-infested, or shallow if we let them. But if we are open to even one 'seed' of change, we can bring forth even from only one stalk a head of grain bearing as many as a hundred new seeds. We can face the many pains and disappointments that come along in a less than perfect world and grow through them into a stronger love for each other. My ambition is to grow old together with my partner.

Communication

An old college professor in America once shocked a conservative audience deeply when he asked them for a four-letter word ending in 'k' that meant 'intercourse'. There was a deadly silence in the lecture hall; no one had the nerve to answer him. At last he smiled kindly over his spectacles and said, 'I know what you're thinking, but the word I'm looking for is 'talk'.

We generally learn patterns of communicating from our own parents. This means that if we've grown up in homes where communication is fragmented—either restricted, stifled, suppressed, or twisted into bouts of fury and hurt—we're likely to communicate in the same destructive ways ourselves. Again, this is where intelligence and maturity comes into play. Can we take time to learn new ways of coping with conflict? It would help, for a start, if we dropped the phrases 'You never...' and 'You always' from our vocabulary, quickly followed by 'I told you so.' We need to be proactive in our conversations, rather than reactive: listening for what's behind a statement rather than for the precise nuances of the words themselves and then jumping to our own defence. In the area of verbal communication, I am now convinced an alarming percentage of Christian families are seriously dysfunctional. Guilt, fear and lack of understanding of modern stress factors, fed by poor role modelling by parents, give rise to frustrated, negative and hasty hostilities in many Christian families. I thank God for a new genre of literature for sincere but fractured families. *Don't Blame Mother* by Paula Caplan (Harper & Row, New York) and *Forgiving our Parents, Forgiving Ourselves* by Dr David Stoop (Servant Publications, Ann Arbour, Michigan), have shed new light on the distress within modern family life—much needed and long overdue.

Sometimes real communication between men and women means loving the other enough to say 'No'—'No' to greed, exploitation, manipulation and erotic idolatry. Then we are also saying 'No' to loneliness, unreal expectations, and the kind of blind romantic idealism that prevents us from knowing wholeness and healing as sexual beings.

When we say 'No' to the distortions of false worship in sexuality, we are saying 'Yes' to real love. There is a desperate need to found relationships on positives, not negatives. Say 'Yes' to what really matters.

7

Violence and Forgiveness

Jesus called the crowd to him and said, 'Listen and understand. What goes into a man's mouth does not make him "unclean", but what comes out of his mouth, that is what makes him "unclean"...Out of the heart come evil thoughts, murder, adultery, sexual immorality, theft, false testimony, slander. These are what makes a man "unclean".'

(Matthew 15:11, 19–20)

Human beings love to persuade themselves that violence is somewhere 'out there', in society. Violence is something we lock in prison or (not seeing our own inconsistency) put in an electric chair. Violence is something drug barons go in for, or the Mafia, or Pol Pot. Violence, we think, is nothing to do with us; and we want nothing to do with it. Jesus had no such illusions. He understood that violence dwells in every human heart. St James echoes his Master's view.

A few years ago there was a hideous case in Australia when a group of young men abducted a beauty queen— picked her up in broad daylight—raped her, slit her throat, and abandoned what was left of her on the side of the road. When they were sentenced to their 'life' imprisonment of eleven years or so, they sat in the front of the court and laughed. I watched clips from the trial on television and thought of Glena and my daughters and felt utterly nauseated. Then I felt furious about all the innocent people who are victims of miscarried justice while guilty ones sit and laugh in court. I found myself wanting to take a gun, tie them up, and shoot them, starting with their feet, until they were full of holes.

I realised, suddenly, with a shock, that there was violence in my own heart as in theirs even if mine was fuelled in part by moral rage. While we have it in us to wreak vengeance and think we're doing ourselves and the victims of savagery a favour, we're in fact only extending the reign of terror. And God doesn't work like that. If one of those brutal murderers wept for what he did to that woman and begged Christ's forgiveness, God would give it lovingly and instantly. The details of violent and sexually insane childhood experiences of the men involved unfolded in a history of warped, dysfunctional, tragic childhood role modelling. The violence had not started with them.

The ugly faces of violence

Violence to women, violence between races and nations— these forms of violence present themselves to us daily on the television news and in newspapers. But what about the less obvious forms of violence that come from within the human heart? It's easy enough to distance ourselves from Serbian, Croatian and Bosnian soldiers battling it out on the streets of what was Yugoslavia; it's easy enough to distance ourselves from US bombing raids on Tripoli or Israeli retribution attacks on Palestinians, or vice versa; it's easy enough to distance ourselves from prostitutes murdered in Amsterdam's red light district; it's easy enough to distance ourselves from massacres in Indonesia or Cambodia...we can do it with the switch of our TV's 'off' button or the flick of a newspaper page to the sports column (not that sport is clear of violence). But, as with any form of pain, we need to confront the violence that's much less obvious and much closer to home.

Do we stop to think, for instance, about the way we speak to our children when we're impatient or irritated with them? Or, on a larger and more insidious scale, do we examine the kind of language we tolerate from the media during a war? During the Gulf War of 1991 the Western press was full of self-congratulatory language about 'brainwashed devils cowering in their foxholes' while 'our boys bravely dug in for battle' and 'our young knights of the skies' inflicted 'collateral damage on the enemy' (theirs, of course, slaughtered ours and did nothing but kill, kill, kill). When Americans fired on British soldiers by accident, miscalculation or incompetence, the attack was described as 'friendly fire'. Somehow, it's acceptable to cover up our own violence with euphemisms, but we certainly don't gloss over the violence of our enemies!

Again, do we stop to think about the violence we let our children (and ourselves!) watch on television? Of course it's part of human nature to be curious about pushing out the boundaries and learning what's beyond a certain threshold. But do we have to sit down under (or in front of) the mental and emotional pollution that pours from Rambo-style videos (all to push the money moguls higher and higher on the hideous pedestals they've erected for themselves or to glamorize the idolatry of nationalism)? Can we any longer ignore the twenty years of studies by researchers at the Philadelphia Annenberg School of Communications that show conclusively the link between television violence and the increase of aggression in society?

And what about the violence that insinuates itself into local football matches? In effect, these become excuses not only for petty vandalism and hooliganism but for the continuation of long-buried tribal differences. We might look back on the pitched battles of pre-Conquest British tribes with disdain, referring to them scornfully as 'quaint skirmishes in the Dark Ages'; but many of the battles fought on and outside football grounds in the 1980s harked back to issues far older than who had the best team— namely, to old prejudices and land disputes between warring tribes more than a thousand years ago. The same must be said, of course, of the so-called 'religious' disputes in Northern Ireland—so close to home for British people, and a source of embarrassed discomfort for the English, but pain and actual death for many Irish people.

Violence is by no means limited to domestic arguments, newspaper editorials, videos, local sporting events, and Belfast. It floods over us from music and musicians, as well. One rock star was once heard to say that sex was like a game of football; you play the game, and once it's over you toss it away, give it the push and forget it. That sentiment is conveyed in song after song that throbs from cassettes, walkmans, and CD players every day. We have grown so anaesthetised to it that we don't even hear the violence any more.

But violence in any form breeds more violence. The only way to break the cycle is to see ourselves as made in God's image. Just as (because we are made in his image) we become outraged at what hurts us and others, so we are capable (again because we are made in his image) of looking beyond the desire for vengeance to the healing of forgiveness and love. If we see the perpetrators of violence, including ourselves, as made in God's image; if we see their personhood instead of just their violence, then we can be a part of God's grace and forgiveness in the world. And unless we do this, we will only be contributing to more violence.

God's image defaced

Violence distorts everything it touches; it disfigures everyone who gives it space, both within and without. It obscures the vision that would otherwise see corruption and exploitation; it hardens hearts that would otherwise feel the softening of compassion and pity; it deafens ears that would otherwise hear cries for mercy; it gives birth to fear that slams doors otherwise open to welcome the needy people of the world.

We cannot afford to be desensitised to violence. If we are in relationship with Jesus, we will never get used to violence. Just because there is no blood on our nice clean carpets when we watch people murdered in Chile or Beijing does not mean we can pretend it's not happening there—or here, in our hearts.

I've had some harsh words for the media so far, as well as our toleration of what they print and broadcast, but occasionally there are journalists and photographers brave enough and prophetic enough to put a stop to violence. Few people will forget the famous Life Magazine photo of a Vietnamese child's naked body burned hideously by napalm during the Vietnam War. Few people will get the image out of their minds from the same senseless war of an officer with his gun at another man's head, about to blow him into eternity. Those two pictures in some ways contributed to the revulsion which ended the Vietnam War, because the moral rage that they aroused swept through the United States with such force that the violence, previously so well concealed, could no longer be tolerated.

The many places of violence

Having said that violence comes from within the human heart, we still need to recognise that the violence beyond our immediate homes and nations is not something we can ignore. It *is* pain, and it *results* in pain—and as we've seen, we ignore pain at our cost. The violence in and around us demands our forgiving response. But we cannot respond if we're ignorant.

Central and South America

Guatemala, El Salvador, Colombia, Nicaragua, Paraguay—how smoothly the poetic Hispanic names roll off the tongue, but how much violence these lands have seen!

In Guatemala and El Salvador, partly because of these countries' proximity to the United States, capitalist governments that represent an elite minority (the gold-plated Mercedes drivers) bill themselves as democrats. In fact both regimes are repressive, propped up by Western governments only because of strategic 'national security' interests—a cover-all term that hides many inequities, brutalities, and forms of corruption. As in the Philippines, where the massive Clark Military Base has stood for America's interests in the Pacific, the two governments here know that their survival depends on supporting the rich first-world nations. Anyone who speaks against the vile and vicious government in either country is imprisoned at best, tortured and murdered by the death squads, or 'disappeared'. But at the very least we in the West should be raising questions about what's happening there.

In Colombia it's the drug barons and the military (uncontrolled by the government) who have driven the country's economy—and also ensured the country's continuing poverty and violence. Life is cheap, at least as far as those who have weapons are concerned. For $20 in Colombia and other Latin American countries, anyone can hire an assassin. 'I want that man taken out.' Just like that! Ghettoes of hate and violence breed yet more hate and violence.

Things haven't been any better in Nicaragua, where the Contras and Sandinistas have battled for power since the dictator Somoza left the country in 1979. When Somoza left he took with him members of the country's National Guard, some of whom came back after Somoza was later murdered in Paraguay (supposedly by left-wing guerillas, but possibly by the dictator of Paraguay, who was alleged to be weary of sheltering him). The National Guard who returned banded together with members of the wealthy classes in Nicaragua who wanted to maintain power and set themselves against the newly formed Sandinista government.

After democratic elections in 1984 the Sandinistas established free health care and education as well as literacy campaigns. The mood of the country was hopeful, but then everything deteriorated again as the Contras, supported by America, continued to fuel internal conflict. Western observers found cruel landmines tagged with pictures of Mickey Mouse planted in the road where children of pro-Sandinistas would walk to school.

In 1991 a coalition government consisting of fourteen fragmented parties with little in common was elected (through American pressure). Violetta Chamarro, who heads the coalition (and has ironically been acclaimed much as Cory Aquino in the Philippines was in the early days), has not been able to govern the country effectively because the unions and the army are still in sympathy with the Sandinistas. In addition, the Contras managed to keep their weapons and have begun a menacing vigilante police force bent on settling old scores through violent reprisals against pro-Sandinistas. The suffering of the poor goes on, especially since wealth is so tightly controlled and limited to the elite few, and inflation gallops along at rampant rates. The West has euphemistically dubbed the Contras 'freedom fighters' but those same 'freedom fighters' have been known to castrate and pierce the eyeballs of peasants who serve the pro-Sandinistas.

It's not hard to see why Somoza escaped to Paraguay. He must have known he was going to a country as brutal and violent as his own—a country where the rich Spanish landowners with their huge haciendas (ranches) violate and do violence to the peasants who farm the land and torture anyone who dares speak against them. The fields of Central and South America are stained with the blood of the poor struggling to eke out a living in a climate of harsh oppression.

The Near East and Africa

The West can no longer turn its back and say 'Not in My Backyard, thanks'. When the Reagan government dropped bombs on Libya in 1986 to warn Gaddafi off, it was signalling to the world its intention to intervene and play world policeman whenever the US government felt it necessary. The same attitude was evident in the Gulf War. No matter how hideously violent the Iraqi government under Saddam Hussein has been, it's not hard to see that the real motive for Western intervention after the invasion of Kuwait had nothing to do with social justice and everything to do with oil.

Christians are as woolly and unjust in their thinking about the age-old Arab/Israeli conflict as they are about what happened in the Gulf. While our sympathies may lie more naturally with the Jewish people because of the church's historic roots in Judaism, this does not mean that we can afford to think in straightforward black/white terms about the Middle-East's agony. Before we swallow too quickly the current platitudes about Israeli rights in what was called Palestine, before we write off Arafat's PLO radicalism, let's at least read Elias Chacour's book *blood Brothers* (Kingsway) or Bill Musk's book *The Unseen face of Islam* (Monarch) and do away with some of our prejudices and ignorances. Without understanding, we are part of the violence ourselves.

The kind of ancient prejudices that inform the on-going violence in the Middle East also inform the terrible bloodshed in South Africa. Baragwanath Hospital in Soweto treats at least 200 people every night, all of whom are there as a result of violence: muggings, gang fights, and apparently motiveless attacks. All the patients are tagged 'critical' or 'urgent', and many die before the over-stretched staff can attend them. Some of the casualties have been injured in the struggle between the warring Inkatha and ANC factions, but many are there simply because Soweto has degenerated into utter chaos; there seems no end to the violence.

But violence is not limited to the cities and townships. As I write, for instance, a prophetic man named Simon Msweli is playing the costly part of a latter-day Robin Hood, trying to defend the rights of a beleaguered Zulu community in Sokhulu. Msweli is in rebellion against the Inkatha-inspired policy (dating back to the release of Nelson Mandela in 1990) of establishing 'homeland' reservations for tribes driven into fear by governments who do not accept the traditional African tribal view that there is no such thing as land ownership. Msweli is leading a group of 300 rebels who are hiding in the forest, fearful of betrayal and reprisal. An *Independent* reporter who met them describes their faces as 'wary, sorrowful and numb', and recounts that there is a 15,000 rand (£3,000) price tag on Msweli's head. Msweli's group have been blamed for murdering people actually murdered by the police. Asked why he is known as 'the Lion of Sokhulu', he answered simply:

> 'Because I tell the truth. Because I always speak the truth.' And what was the truth? 'Inkatha is behind all this. The chief and his headman...they want our land and they also want to eliminate the ANC—to drive us out or kill us...And the Inkatha chief also wants the land of my family...I must stay here to protect the people. If I leave, they can die.'
>
> (*Independent*, 27 May 1992)

Meanwhile, Archbishop Desmond Tutu has been branded a Communist for daring to prophesy that there will be more massacres and pogroms in South Africa unless real justice comes for the blacks—not just storefront window-dressing to please aid-giving, trading Western governments.

The Far East

The atrocities of the Pol Pot regime in Cambodia still leave the world in a cold sweat of fear and horror. At their height, Pol Pot and his death squads used to line up young men who resisted his regime, castrate them, force them to eat their genitals, then while they were screaming in agony shoot them. This was a madman, the likes of whom the world hasn't seen since Hitler's deathcamps, whom some Western nations actually supported...for the crazy reasoning that he was against the USSR. I do not ignore the madness, now so apparent to the world, of Communist atrocities in Romania or across what once was the Soviet Union. I only underscore the fact that the West has supported so much violence in the other camps out of self interest and ideology also.

But the stories of violence aren't always so horrific. There's another story from the Philippines which has travelled across the world recently. Late one night an Australian priest, Fr Brian Gore, was greeted at his door by a man trembling with fear and anxiety. 'They're coming to take my land tomorrow,' he said. Fr Brian was horrified. He had been in the Philippines long enough to know that this man's family, while never wealthy had, as peasant farmers, farmed their sugar plantation faithfully for generations. Now the authorities, who saw how well the land had been cared for, wanted the land for themselves and were coming to take it by force.

Fr Brian thought for a few minutes and told the man to gather a few friends and relatives. 'I'll meet you in the morning just before they come,' he promised. That night, however, he hardly slept. He knew there would be bloodshed, and he knew he should be standing at the forefront to defend the family about to lose the farm. He was terrified himself.

When he arrived at the plantation the next morning his mouth dropped open with surprise. The land and the surrounding hillside were a sea of people—ten thousand had gathered in protest about what was to happen. Men, women, children, old men on crutches and babes in arms were all there. The farmer had tears of joy and bewilderment in his eyes as he greeted Fr Brian, and suddenly the priest's fear left him. A man of peace, he was convinced now that he should be the first to stand in front of the jeeps that were rolling in on the farm; that if he did not do so he would never again be able to stand in front of his congregation and proclaim 'This is the gospel of the Lord'.

He committed his life into God's hands as the first jeep, heavily armed, rolled nearer. He went forward. 'Are you going to shoot every one of us?' he challenged. 'Because until you leave this plantation alone, not one of us will budge.' Then, before he had a chance to say more, an old woman rushed out of the crowd, her grandchild in her arms. Pointing at a soldier on the nearest jeep, she shrieked in outrage at him, 'What do you think you're doing? You're a disgrace to your family, sitting up there like a great baby playing with a wicked toy like that and taking away innocent people's land. Why, I remember when you were no bigger than this baby here, yourself. Shame on you!'

There was a moment of terrible silence when Fr Brian knew things could go either way. Rifles were raised, and tempers were running high. But a woman's outrage is stronger than a man's weaponry. The young soldier hung his head, and, to the stunned amazement of everyone in the crowd, dropped his rifle and machine gun, got off the jeep, entered the crowd and turned to face his former colleagues. One by one the jeeps hesitated, and eventually all the soldiers left. As far as Fr Brian was concerned, there was a feeling of immense relief! And as far as the farmer and his friends were concerned, there had been a miracle. Violence had been met with the loving rebuke of a huge Filipino 'family' who commanded more loyalty and love than any orders to kill, and who had the courage to break the circle of violence by meeting it with peace.

Whether we like it or not, whether we see it or not, the world's pain and violence are in our backyards, because the world is our backyard; we are part of a global family. When we bemoan the horrors of bloodbaths in countries 'over there', let's remember that there is a different kind of violence right in our own backyards—in Canberra, Whitehall, and Washington. It is a violence which gives the casual shrug or nod to other violence, or sometimes even calculates it with bloodless coldness. Political violence is in no way better than any other form of physical violence, especially as its effects reach so far.

Racial violence

I decided a long time ago that when I meet God in heaven there are several questions I'm going to ask. The first are these: why, why have black people suffered out of all proportion to their numbers on this planet? Why has racism been allowed to wreak all the havoc it has wrought? Why is it that black people and white people in the West are like two groups with a massive plate-glass window between them: looking at each other, their mouths working at each other, but neither hearing the other? And what makes many whites think they are superior?

Racism is not a social error. It is a heresy based on a misunderstanding of God's creative work in the human race; it is a marring of God's image in human beings; it is a serious, vicious, wicked sin. Every human being was created in the image of God, and he has placed his stamp as much on the black baby born in Soweto as he has on the white baby who until the dismantling of apartheid hoped for automatically grows up with the exclusive right to vote or rule—just because of the colour of his skin. Under apartheid, even an albino gorilla has more chance of becoming president than a man whose skin bore black pigment. Likewise, anyone who believed in the theory of evolution was not permitted to teach in a South African school; but it was apparently OK to drive black people off the best beaches because the dark colour of their skin was an offence against the pristine whiteness of the sand. Apartheid is an obscenity, and the human race bears its scars! Its spirit is duplicated in more subtle forms in the ghettos of USA and in the fringe-dwelling communities of impoverished Aboriginal camps in Australia. No serious moral thinker could take President Bush's public statements about the '92 riots in Los Angeles seriously when he denied that the causes were racial oppression and poverty, arguing rather that they were simply the activities of street gangs.

Those who are insecure about their identity are more likely to be caught up in racial violence than those who are not. They can't forgive others for having a different skin colour or tilt of the eyes or curl of the hair. In their fear and ignorance, then, they turn to violence as a solution. (Hitler even called it the 'final solution'—a fine piece of wording for one of the ugliest crimes this planet has ever witnessed in the holocaust of six million Jews, gypsies and dissidents.)

God understood this kind of unforgiveness, giving us the story of the army captain who was healed of leprosy (2 Kings 5:1–17). Lepers would have abounded in those times, yet God chose to heal a Syrian soldier and so call into question the assumed righteousness of the Hebrews who might have thought they somehow had a monopoly on God's healing powers. When Jesus confronted the racist basis for discrimination in Jewish thinking by reviewing that story in Luke 4:25–30, the 'church-attending' synagogue crowd violently rose up and took him to a hill top to kill him. 'They meant to throw him over a cliff.' What violence racism engenders—even to the point of attempted assassination of the Prince of Peace!!

Of course God's Son also understood this kind of unforgiveness, illustrating it in his healing of the ten lepers (see Luke 17:11–19). Of the ten, nine were Jewish and gave him no thanks. The tenth was a Samaritan—feared and hated by the pious Jews for being one of a race that had married 'foreign' women and in some cases had forgotten God altogether. His commendation of the one Samaritan who did give thanks was not just to illustrate the importance of thanksgiving but to cut straight to the heart of racism—the kind of racism that often dwells in the heart that most prides itself on 'holiness'! A parallel today would be if Jesus healed ten people with AIDS: nine paid up members of the Conservative party who worshipped at their local Anglican and House Churches, and one Iraqi, a former henchman of Saddam Hussein. Wouldn't the hackles go up!

Racial prejudice, like any other form of violence, lives in all our hearts. At the time of the birth of Christ, shepherds (like tax collectors and lepers) were social outcasts, much as gypsies are today in France, Britain or Portugal. What a scandal then for the Jews of the day that the first people invited to the manger in Bethlehem were shepherds from the fields! What a scandal for the Greek- and Roman-influenced Jews that a carpenter's kid born in a stable, living the life of a fugitive, owning no property or land, should claim to be God's Son—then die, beaten and naked, on an ignominious Roman form of the gallows!

People are still easily scandalised today. Witness what happened once in the Middle East when Melbourne's late Anglican archbishop, Dr David Penman, was giving Communion in the cathedral. (He recounted the story afterwards, so I heard it first hand.) It so happened that the first in the queue to receive Communion was a man who had just been converted—at great personal cost and danger—from Islam to the Christian faith. As soon as the congregation saw that this former Moslem had touched the platter of bread and drunk from the cup of wine at the Lord's table, they refused to go forward and share in the Communion themselves.

Many Christians are racist, some of them without even realising it because their racism has soaked in through the pores of their environment and is deeply entrenched. I know this is true because I was racist myself, fed on the fundamentalist teachings of American preachers from the Deep South—men like John Rice and Bob Jones. At one time I even preached in public that Martin Luther King was a womanising, communist heretic planted by the devil to deceive believers—until a Christian friend challenged me to read a book of King's sermons, *Strengthen to Love*, and all my prejudices were turned upside down.

One American Bible College, which I considered attending in the earlier (fundamentalist) years of my spiritual pilgrimage was an example of the extraordinary ethics of some such groups. The college barred blacks from entry. Then, cynically, when the state and federal authorities told the university that it would receive no more tax benefits once the desegregation laws were operational (after King's energetic work on behalf of American blacks), the university reversed its decision to disallow blacks. Suddenly it was 'God's will' that they permit the entrance of black students—as long as they developed no romantic attachments to white women—in which case they were dismissed.

Similarly, flag-draped coffins and body bags, first from Vietnam, then from the Falklands, and later from the Gulf War, usually backed up with photographs and movies of weeping white middle-class parents, hide the fact that far more black soldiers lost their lives in that war than white. The nice white college boys got deferments and arranged draft dodges, but the blacks had fewer options and wound up facing the Vietcong mortar attacks as they defended villages whose names they did not know in a war they frequently did not understand.

Old prejudices die hard, and (at the risk of sounding anti-Semite at a time when, happily, it's **not** OK to be anti-Semite), I want to add one more story to illustrate the truth of that fact. I was once on a bus going into Israel from Egypt, where I had just visited the Pyramids and the Sphinx and marvelled at the creativity and vision of the ancient Egyptians. At the Israeli border, the bus drivers changed over and I went forward to ask the new driver, 'Can you drink the water up here?' The Israeli bus tour guide looked disgusted. 'Young man,' he said (never mind that I was 45 at the time!), 'in case you aren't aware of it, you have just entered civilisation.' And with a smirk he glanced back at Egypt, then ahead into his homeland of Israel. I had to bite my tongue to stop myself from replying my thoughts: 'Old man, let me remind you that when your mob were still running around the wilderness chasing sheep and goats, the Egyptians were constructing buildings of such might and splendour that even now their architecture defies full understanding and explanation.'

Racism is a foul, stinking offence in the nostrils of God. We need to face it in ourselves, to face the violence it engenders, then to seek God's healing forgiveness. As we shall see in a moment, we also need to learn from Jesus' response to those of other races how, forgiven ourselves, we can forgive others for being different; can even rejoice in the differences!

Violence to women

A second group of questions I'd like to ask God when I reach heaven concerns the lot of women in history. I remember reading Susan Brownmiller's book *Against Our Will*, after which I wept over my male identity for days and wished I had not been born a man, because of the generations of shame and degradation men had heaped on women. I want to ask God why women have suffered so much. While men in affluent countries fall into squabbles over whether their next company car should be a Porsche or a Volvo, Serbian soldiers in Bosnia and Croatia rape the womenfolk of their Slavic cousins just as brutally as Australians and Americans raped Vietnamese women in the Vietnam War. And behind the facade of fine suburban houses, respectable citizens oppress and sexually violate both spouses and children.

Much, but not all, of the violence of men against women arises from men's frustration with the advances of women. Where men have scarcely changed in their attitudes over the last three decades, women have moved on with courage to stand against assumptions of their weakness and incompetence in business, industry, and education. Women look like a terrible threat to their menfolk, and men, facing their own weakness honestly (and perhaps for the first time in history) tremble with the need to reassert their power and control over women.

No one profile fits a rapist: he may be a white-collar commuter with too many unpaid bills; he may be a university student bettered repeatedly by female classmates; he may be from a ghetto or from a boardroom. Wherever he's from, his choice to rape often has nothing or little to do with his sex drive, and everything to do with a violent impulse to suppress and belittle women. Sociologists are meanwhile showing with convincing statistics that men under stress—including the 'stress' of women's greater freedom and self-expression—are more likely because of insecurity and anger to react to women in a violent or perverted way. It's not just that men have become more wicked, but that in a society robbed of a spiritual heart, the Christian ideals of servanthood, love, and communication are lost in the flood of male hormones.

Music, as we have seen, sometimes fuels the fire of violence of men against women. It amazes me that in an era when women are speaking out in self-defence, no one seems to say anything about the way women are depicted in the videos that tout current rock musicians' work. Women are no longer portrayed merely as sex kittens, 1930s style, all coyness and flashing eyes as they dance with men—as if that image weren't bad enough. But nowadays sado-masochism expressed (not always subtly) through gesture, clothing, posture, and the words of the songs themselves invades popular culture as a cruel tide of accepted perversion.

One reason that domination of women goes on and is even encouraged in some religious circles is that the New Testament teaching of male headship of the family has been drastically misunderstood and misapplied and taken out of the context of nurturing, protecting and forgiving love that Christ lived and taught. The verse that commands women to obey their husbands is bandied about like a blunt sword, totally out of line with the huge weight of teaching on justice; totally out of line with Jesus' solidarity with broken women who had been prostitutes, bleeding women who had been outcast. Two thousand years ago, when the father of the family said jump, the woman said 'How high?'—and leapt for it! But many countries, including my own, have not yet caught up with much of the rest of the world in realising that things have changed; that men and women may be different but they are nevertheless equally created in God's image.

We need therefore to get away from the old misinterpretations of Scripture and publicly take a stand against violence to women.

Some time ago a group, then named 'Men Against Sexual Assault' was formed in Australia. I hastened to join, in a desire to see men stand up to their own in a position of justice and peace. Some criticism of this group has caused me to question the motivation, but certainly **not** the principles of this initiative. A purely feminist reactionary response may in the end be divisive and breed male insecurity and prejudice but there is a desperate need for Christian men to stand with their sisters in the struggle for justice. This is the very least we can do (as well as dealing with our own confused and twisted attitudes to the role of women) if we have the nerve to pray 'Thy Kingdom come'—a prayer for the heaven where there is no rape, no crying, no incest: no pain for women or men.

Incest—even the word is taboo in most churches. But wherever I go I meet young men who have scarred their sisters with incest; young women—and men—who have been raped by their fathers and uncles and brothers. One Australian woman told me a story that probably represents only the tip of a hideous iceberg that threatens to ram a hole in Christian witness and relationships generally. She had gone to the pastors of her local church to get help against the brutality of her husband. The pastors stood there like cowards while her husband did a demonstration of his 'headship'. He ripped the phone off the wall and smashed her face with it, right in front of them. Then he beat her right arm so violently that she couldn't have lifted the phone to call for further help, even if the phone had been working. When the woman pleaded again with the pastors, they turned away saying that the husband's behaviour was nothing they could control, as he was the head of the house.

The woman was desperate because she believed that

unless her husband committed adultery she could not leave him. The pastors knew something that they did not discuss that day as they left her to her beating; that she had other grounds for leaving her husband, because he had been repeatedly raping their son, a boy by then squeezed dry of all feeling, all hope, all sense of meaning in life. Desperately, the woman told her husband she would go on television to tell her story. 'You would bring discredit to the name of Jesus,' he told her. 'I forbid you to do that—it's flat rebellion if you do.' This, in spite of the fact that the father admitted to the acts of sexual violation.

I was incensed as I listened to her tale. Nothing the woman had done brought discredit to Jesus, but that man had more than marred Christ's image in his poor wife and suffering son. And all in the name of 'theology'. Further counselling of the boy indicated that he is so severely damaged that only a miracle can restore him to a healthy life. The Christian church must clear its decks and openly deal with these issues. 'The time has come for judgement to begin and God's own people are the first to be judged' (1 Peter 4:17).

Jesus' response to violence

All violence—whether to children, the poor, women, or those of other races—is pornographic. it is more so when it is justified by the application of God's 'law'. Jesus' treatment of a woman caught in the act of adultery (see John 8:3–11) laid to rest once and for all the supposed right of 'holy' people to rely on their own righteousness in dealing out violence to 'unholy' people. While the Pharisees rubbed their hands in anticipation of seeing the woman stumble and fall under the crushing weight of huge stones thrown 'legally' at her for her sins, Jesus calmly told them that unless they were free from sin, they could throw nothing. Only he himself was free from sins;

only he could therefore justifiably hurl a stone. But he didn't.

Instead, he forgave her, telling her only to change her way of life. Mind you, the gentleness of Jesus towards female sexual 'offenders' has within it the reality of women's powerlessness in Hebrew culture. The sexually oppressed deserve our strongest commitment to justice.

Jesus was never violent in his judgements. Unlike the now blow-dried and handsomely suited Ku Klux Klan in America (the old druidic white-clad image has gone underground these days), Jesus returned gentleness for violence. In Gethsemane, for instance, when his impulsive friend Peter cut off the ear of the high priest's servant, Jesus rebuked him, healed the servant and challenged the violent men who had come to arrest him. If ever violence was justifiable in response to violence, the protection of Jesus was the ultimate justifiable force. Notice the long list of people who had banded together to make the arrest; their insecurity in creating such an alliance in itself tells a tale of violent hearts:

> But Jesus answered, 'No more of this!' And he touched the man's ear and healed him. Then Jesus said to the chief priests, the officers of the temple guard, and the elders, who had come for him, 'Am I leading a rebellion, that you have come with swords and clubs? Every day I was with you in the temple courts, and you did not lay a hand on me. But this is your hour—when darkness reigns.'
>
> (Luke 22:51–53)

No wonder Jesus was subjected to the ultimate and most horrific sentence that could be meted out in Roman Judea: he was a threat to the powerbase of the time! He must have been—why else would anyone nail to a piece of wood a man who was loving to children, respectful to women, and not only preached doing good but went about healing and helping the downtrodden?

'Love your enemies.' Jesus' words were uncompromising. We laugh about 'turning the other cheek' and sharing our coat with someone who takes us to court for our shirt, but for Jesus it was no laughing matter. We are to pray for those who are cruel to us and to others—whether we love those others or not. It doesn't matter if our 'enemies' are in Iraq or Libya, the IRA or Indonesia, Serbia or Central America, we are to pray for them. Jesus has abolished once and for all the notion that anyone has the right to take life from another either in vengeance or punishment; only God has that prerogative. In carrying violence to a violent end on the cross, Jesus' response was so simple, yet so hard for us to accept: 'Father, forgive them, for they do not know what they are doing' (Luke 23:34).

Somehow, we who call ourselves Christ's servants must learn to face the violence in and around us and hold mercy and forgiveness in tension with justified outrage at the actions of violent people. Our sense of moral indignation too often betrays us into more violence, but we need to see, through the Holy Spirit's help, that even violent people have been made in God's image; we need to see through the violence to the creative love of God for them. Forgiveness is the only way.

Jesus, on the cross, absorbed the violence of human history. As the salt is destroyed in the process of absorbing the bitterness of the olive, so must we be a community which takes into our own body—even to the extent of self-giving—the task of being salt of the earth.

We are faced again and again by our own lonely, unpopular Gethsemane. Not our wilfullness but the will of the Prince of Peace is the order of our violent planet's day.

8

Art in the Analgesic Society

In Chapter 4 we thought about the work of musicians like Charlie Bird Parker, U2, Tchaikovsky, Handel, and Beethoven. But jazz, rock, and classical musicians are not the only ones whose art comes out of pain. Poets, novelists, painters and filmmakers down the years have shared similar experiences.

Take Samuel Taylor Coleridge. Dispatched to boarding school while still a small boy, he suffered acute loneliness. Depression dogged him into adult life, and in the end drugs also twisted his mind. Still, some of the most moving poetry in the English language came out of his tortured imagination—poems about both dejection and joy; poems about dark unhappiness and bright, beautiful things that gave praise to God.

Twentieth-century Welsh poet Dylan Thomas knew some of the same anguish and addiction, though the causes were different. Rather than loneliness, it was the acute pain of the discrepancy between his public face and his private emotions that hurt him. Alcohol offered him the oblivion he longed for, and in the end he died of his alcoholism while on a lecture tour in America. In spite of all, however, he left a collection of poems that celebrates the wonder of creation and the joy of life—as well as poems that bemoaned his bewilderment about the harshness of that same life.

Novelist Charles Dickens faced his pain with greater apparent success than these two poets. While Dickens was a boy, his father lurched crazily from one financial catastrophe to another. Dickens was therefore haunted by his experiences of the debtors' prison and with having to go to work in a shoe-blacking factory as a child. Images of imprisonment and childhood pain drove him to write prophetically and with indignation about the sufferings of children like Oliver Twist, David Copperfield and Nicholas Nickleby. And although his own adult relationships bore the marks of his childhood difficulties, he was often able to transmute the experiences into laughter for his readers. He had confronted the pain, and he let his writing be a channel for overcoming it.

Some painters in the last two centuries worked out their pain on the canvas. Toulouse Lautrec, a man stunted in body but with eyes of compassion for the lot of prostitutes and the poor in France, painted with such passion that to look at his paintings is to ask—as readers of Dickens must inevitably ask now—how the people of his day suffered as much as they did, and how the people who might have changed things could have remained so indifferent. Debauched, promiscuous, and ugly—a flawed prophet if ever there was one—Toulouse Lautrec nevertheless made a towering contribution to Impressionist and later painters.

Van Gogh was another painter who was intimate with pain. Exposed as a young man to noxious glue gases from a shoeshop adjacent to his lodgings, Van Gogh almost certainly suffered some sort of brain dysfunction. His obsession with the colour yellow, and with the contrast between yellow and black in his paintings of crow-covered cornfields, starry nights and sunflowers, shows his hunger for finding light in dark places. His legacy is enormous.

Rejected in his passionate attempts to care for the poor as a radical evangelist, Vincent suffered at the hands of a pharisaical conservative school of evangelism where the leaders, rather than enriching and empowering him, drove him to despair and loss of faith.

Art is undoubtedly a way that some people have of expressing their pain. In days when communities are scattered, families and marriages broken, and house-moves almost as frequent for many as for ancient nomadic tribes, artists have sung, played, written and painted their pain in an effort to make sense of it without necessarily reaching for other more destructive analgesics—though some (like Coleridge and Thomas) did both.

In 1988 in Nicaragua I visited a woman and her daughter whose paintings have caught the imagination of Latin America and beyond. Their work is both political and religious, though it would shock conservative Christians with its political boldness. In one painting, for example, the mother shows Jesus' crucifixion in a modern context with the CIA clustered at the foot of the cross, hard hats on and guns held at the ready.

I asked the daughter about a rumour I had heard that she was visiting the Nicaraguan prisons and teaching imprisoned Contras—her enemies, and the murderers of her brother—how to produce art in this form. 'Why don't you only tell them about the love of Jesus?' I asked.

'You don't understand,' she told me. 'Many of us Sandinistas who are Christians in this country fought against Somoza because of his vicious wickedness—and his oppression of our people. We long for our brothers and sisters who still fight against us now to be gathered in, to be loved. We don't want to take it out on them. We don't want them to suffer any more. We want the internal war to end, and we long for a day when we embrace one another. We will paint pictures of a new kingdom together. How we long for that day! But in the meantime we go to the prisons and teach those who killed and tortured our loved ones how to draw and paint. That way, when they are released, there will be a restoration of relationships. Our paintings—done together—will help restore complete peace to this broken country.'

The art of those two women is the kind of art an analgesic society needs. It is the art of forgiveness and reconciliation. It is the art of honesty about pain—not just escape from pain. In the end, therefore, it is the art that ministers healing and wholeness to us.

Art as a threat

One Easter our church in Melbourne decided to mount an exhibition of photographs of some of the great works of art that depict Jesus on the cross. The collection varied widely: everything from gorgeous and dramatic Renaissance pictures of Christ dying against Italian landscapes surrounded by European peasants, to starkly modern, symbolic pictures. One showed the carcass of a sheep, flayed and hanging on a butcher's hook. Its imagery of the slaughter-house was too much for some folk in the congregation, but the picture was (to my mind at least) an honest attempt to capture the horror and cost of Jesus' sacrifice for us.

One thing I noticed as I looked around at the pictures was that in all but one of them Jesus was shown with a loincloth discreetly draped around him so that the viewers couldn't see a full-frontal view of his body. I was intrigued by that one picture and asked several people in the church how they felt about it. A few were offended, but I thought as I looked at Jesus in that picture of the full meaning of those verses in John's gospel which for most Christians have in themselves an almost cultic sacredness about them, read as they are in thousands of churches around the world at Christmas each year:

In the beginning was the Word, and the Word was with God, and the Word was God. He was with God in the beginning. Through him all things were made; without him nothing was made that has been made. In him was life, and that life was the light of men.... The Word became flesh and made his dwelling among us. We have seen his glory, the glory of the One and Only, who came from the Father, full of grace and truth.

(John 1:1–14)

Somehow—and this notion is quite foreign to the gospel, and certainly foreign to the Father who sent his Son— we have 'sanitised' Jesus. Our thinking, and therefore our art, still leans towards the heresy that Jesus was above being human. With this twisted vision, we unconsciously try to rob him of the full-frontal humanity the Father gave him in his earthly flesh; we rob him of his gender and his potential sexuality; we reduce our own understanding of his care for us as creative human beings; we reduce the loving demand that he represents on our lives, emasculating him. As a result, we emasculate our faith and enter the realm of warm fuzzies at the expense of raw, full-bodied faith that raises questions and offers answers for every part of our lives on earth.

Perhaps those who were offended by a nude Jesus unconsciously recognised the power of art to make us confront unpalatable truths. Perhaps, too, this capacity of art is precisely what makes it so threatening to self-righteous and powerful people. Art is prophetic, and as such it will evoke the same mixed response of wonder, fear, and shame as any other form of prophecy.

A doctor in Paraguay wanted to speak peace to the violence he saw and experienced on a daily basis. He was a Christian man who served the peasants with unflagging devotion, and he was weary and outraged by the treatment meted out to peasants by the right-wing regime in Paraguay. One day he decided to create pictures of what he had seen in his medical work. He portrayed faces stained with tears, bodies twisted by torture, defenceless peasants with their hearts not on their 'sleeves' but screwed to the outside of their bodies as a sign of Paraguay's suffering and heart-woundedness. Behind the peasants he showed the pathetic little hovels they inhabited against the background of the rich Spanish haciendas; and he also showed in the background the greed-driven ugliness of the landowners who persecuted the peasants to their early deaths. He spared no detail.

The secret police heard of his pictures and sought him out. 'You stop that kind of art, or you'll be very sorry,' they warned him. But he went on with his work.

Soon after the warning the secret police came for the doctor's sixteen-year-old son. They wired him up with clamps for electric shocks attached to his genitals, mutilated him, and tortured him until he died. Then they abandoned him on a blood-soaked mattress on the street...where his father found him.

The doctor looked pain in the face as he had done so many times before—but never so acutely. He thought fleetingly of the pomp and circumstance of a traditional funeral with a made-up face and waxed body to show serenity in death, and he rejected the lie of it. Instead, he took his son's broken body and laid it on the same blood-stained mattress at the door of the cathedral so that everyone who walked past it—including members of the secret police still attending church—would see it.

He did that for two reasons: he wanted to show (as his pictures were already showing) that the killings, maimings and torturings of Paraguay were marring God's image not just for the individuals who suffered, but for the whole country. His action was a cry of protest against all that was dehumanising in the power-games of that right-wing government. It was a statement against oppression and sin, but it was also a statement of hope. 2000 years ago another Father displayed the tortured, broken body of his Son on a public cross for all to see. Like the divine Father, this man had taken his son and displayed him and his suffering for all the world to see as a sign that God will never leave us nor forsake us; by his wounds, healing comes into the world.

The paradox of good art is that it gives both artist and society more power (of perception and wonder), yet at the same time its power opens both artist and society to vulnerability and even danger. In the wrong hands—as we've seen in the lives of many rock musicians who have abused their art for their own greedy ends—art is destructive. Perhaps this is why many in society, especially in the church, fear, mistrust and in the end reject art. The Puritans could not cope with the prophetic demands of seventeenth-century satire, so, pointing the finger at some of the excesses and crudities in contemporary theatre, they rejected all dramatic art and with one fell swoop closed all English theatres in 1642. Things haven't changed much in three hundred years! In Communist countries before the fall of the Iron Curtain, poets and writers were imprisoned and silenced—among them Irina Ratushinskaya and Alexander Solzhenitsyn—because their work was judged by the authorities to represent a threat to the 'stability' of the Communist government.

The arts rejected

We can easily distance ourselves from that kind of repression, but the Christian church has in many cases hung if not an Iron Curtain then at least a linen cloth across art that would tell the truth. Painters, sculptors, musicians, playwrights and novelists are still suspect, still regarded as dissident, 'unscriptural', 'liberal', or beyond the pale. The problem lies partly in some Christians' prejudice about the role of art in society. For many Christians, art should be a vehicle of direct evangelisation; they cannot comprehend the indirect and understated or implied faith or prophecy of the artists. They resent the fact that the art doesn't spell out in block capitals 'JESUS SAVES', that it doesn't have Scripture verses written boldly in every corner.

How blind that expectation is! We don't expect a Christian doctor to hang up a sign outside his surgery saying 'I believe in God, Father Almighty, Maker of heaven and earth, and in Jesus Christ...' We choose a doctor because he is a good doctor who cares about his patients and helps to heal them. Similarly, we can't expect artists to trumpet orthodox faith from every corner of their plays, paintings, and novels. We need to see instead that many artists' vision is completely shot through with the love and wonder of God and his creation (even if unacknowledged) and with a keen perception of pain; we need to see that their art can plant a seed of faith in the questioning onlooker or reader.

Art and preaching simply don't mix; when art becomes too polemic, it ceases to be art. It becomes mere propaganda! We need to liberate artists from the false shackles of our short-sighted expectations. Not only that, but we need to encourage them and enjoy their work without the prejudices that consign all art to obscurity at best and Satan at worst. We need to see that art is part of God's redeeming work in the world today. Likewise it is the convulsing nerve ends of a broken world.

Even if the church goes on rejecting art—whether created by Christian or by other artists—art will continue to be one of God's vehicles for prophetic truth. We have been too limited in our expectations of the ways in which God works; we try to narrow God's capacity to change hearts to the work of words from pulpits, words from teaching books, and words from the Scriptures. God certainly uses those means, but he is the God of the Word made flesh, as well. He also has a far richer storehouse than many in the church want to recognise, and many artists are winnowing hard in the harvest fields!

Truth leaks out through art whether we accept and recognise it or not: in drama, sculpture, novels, paintings and films. Recalling the prophet Habakkuk, Jesus told his friends that if people won't speak the truth, even ordinary stones will cry it out: 'The stones of the wall will cry out, and the beams of the woodwork will echo it' (Habakkuk 2:11).

Woody Allen as prophet and filmmaker

I'd like to look at the work of Woody Allen in the context of Acts chapter 17. The relevance of one to the other will soon be clear if you read that chapter, for Woody Allen offers the same kind of challenge to the world as the Athenian statues and poetry offered to the men of Athens if they could see it. For Paul, interpretation rather than rejection of art was the demanding task of the preacher.

When Peter preached to the Jews in Jerusalem on the Day of Pentecost, the effects were dramatic: three thousand people gave their lives to Christ in faith (see Acts 2). By contrast, when Paul preached to the Athenians, most sneered, and few believed. It would be easy, therefore, to dismiss the artistry of Paul's preaching as inferior to Peter's…easy, but mistaken. The value of any creative work—whether reasoned preaching or artistic endeavour—cannot necessarily be measured by the size or response of the audience.

Peter's message was so well received because the Jews' hearts had been prepared for generations by the Holy Spirit to receive it. Basically, what Peter was saying in Jerusalem was what they had waited to hear since the earliest Old Testament times: they had awaited a Messiah, and now here he was; all they had to do was put their trust in Jesus Christ. He was speaking to them in a language and with imagery they would understand; it was the language of Zion. No wonder there were so many converts!

The situation in Athens, however, was altogether different. Paul was preaching on Mars Hill, in the shadow of a once-great civilisation now in the shadows of Roman conquest. No receptive Jewish faces looking back at Paul here, but a crowd of hardened intellectuals who had seen it all, done it all, heard it all before. Like Woody Allen in his film *Manhattan*, Paul had to reach across the wilderness of blasé, world-weary attitudes into people's hearts and souls. And he could do this because he was well educated in Hellenistic thought, and (as we can see from his many writings) had a keen understanding of Greek art and culture. He knew only too well the Greek philosophers' penchant for asking and debating thorny questions. He knew only too well that they tolerated him just because he was saying something new and different, not because he was carrying the Christian gospel, per se.

Paul had to meet the Athenians where they were. Some of his listeners called themselves 'Epicurians', and some of them 'Stoics'. The Epicurians, followers of the Greek philosopher Epicurus, believed that the highest good is personal happiness and its sensual quest. By contrast the Stoics, followers of another Greek philosopher, Zeno, believed that the highest good consists of virtue and control of one's feelings and passions. The debates and questions were perpetual, an end in themselves for these Athenians.

Like Paul we are living in a culture that is giving up on its old values. Whereas Peter was securely within the Jewish enclave when he preached, Paul had stepped out of it and into a pre-Christian culture. Peter didn't have to address the painful questions of the Jews simply because there weren't so many of them. Paul on the other hand stood before a crowd of sceptics for whom 'Jesus is the answer' would have been a ridiculous piece of obscure theology; the Greeks' reply would have been 'Never mind the answer! What's the question?' So Paul didn't want to shy away from their painful questions and took the risk of engaging the Athenians on their own ground; he studied the sculptures on Mars Hill and began his remarks by talking about Greek art—a language they would all understand.

Woody Allen, 'prophesying' to Manhattan and beyond, is doing much the same thing. Like Paul an acute watcher of culture, he sees in Western urban life in general, and in himself in microcosm, all the emptiness of a new kind of wilderness spreading into a dying culture; the materialism and hedonism of the Epicurians, and the worldly moralism of the Stoics, neither of which outlook could offer healing and help to the human heart.

Paul was a man of immense intelligence who could easily have courted the kind of acclaim Greek philosophers of previous generations had won for themselves in Athens. Instead, he directed them to the altar of their 'unknown God' and thence to the Lord Jesus.

Woody Allen, similarly, could easily have received the veneration and idolatry of filmgoers and many others in the West, but he has shunned it, always subordinating himself to his art. He seems to have an intrinsic sense, possibly partly arising from the context of his Jewish upbringing, that his identity lies in something beyond his own and his actors' performance. He is primarily a creative man, very much alive, not hung up on his own image; enjoying his art but apparently free from the false idolatry that it might create in him.

A feature of his life and art that makes an interesting commentary on a Christian view of the arts is that Allen— unlike the Christian greetings-card artists with their chocolate-box view of the world—is unafraid to face and portray pain. He observes our culture's brokenness and vulnerability; he observes society's hunger for questions—and through laughter he makes us face all these things. Portrayed by the media as tormented workaholic, reclusive and neurotic, Allen is in fact extraordinarily clear-sighted and well balanced. He enjoys his work but is not obsessed with it. He says that he sometimes envies religious people their faith, but that he can't cope with all the 'hassles' of organised religion. However, he also says that it would never occur to him that the universe was not without meaning—and it's that meaning, and the search for it, which he wants to convey in his films. He has an ear, in fact, for the voice of God—even if unacknowledged and unnamed—resonating through the world.

Woody Allen appears not to have sold out to the self-congratulation which many who would call themselves Christians espouse. But he has certainly tapped into the wonder of God's creation and the puzzles of human relationships in a world that makes an idol of them because of the absence of true worship.

If only Christian artists would have so uncluttered and brave a vision! Why is it that while Christians carry on what in many cases has become a charade of family and church life, Woody Allen, without faith, faces the pain, sees the farce, and asks the questions? In that sense, Woody Allen is following in the footsteps of Paul on Mars Hill.

We can sneer from our lofty evangelical height if we want to, but we do so at our own peril. Like the Stoics, we are dualistic regarding the physical world. We are also too afraid of our feelings. We are therefore in hideous danger of reduction into uncreative beings with agendas far too limited and attitudes far too censorious. We are in danger of ceasing to reflect the poetic, artistic, creative nature of the God whose image we say we bear.

We can't afford these attitudes any more than we can afford to neglect or ignore art.

Art and creativity

Art is more inspired by a spiritual quest than by anything else—more even than by eroticism or human relationships. Egyptian pyramids and Druid stone circles tried to make sense of the mysteries of the universe. Byzantine art reflected in its delicate and detailed mosaics the longing for God. Mediaeval architecture soared and reached for God. Renaissance painting celebrated the closeness of God to the life of ordinary people. Modern literature has agonised over the supposed absence of God. Art, in fact, is God-obsessed—whether the artist acknowledges God or not. This is what makes creativity so important for Christians.

Creativity is not however to be confused with the kind of false artistic endeavour that glorifies itself at the expense of God. Just as sexual greed represents the opposite of true worship, so false artistic endeavour congratulates itself and draws the audience away from the prophetic vision, perception, and truth that might otherwise come from it. But to reject all art just because some forms of art are corrupt is to miss so much that God must long for us to see and hear. On the other hand it is true that, as one celebrated Australian arts commentator observed, one cannot always justify art for its structure alone when its message is dangerous. A toilet seat magnificently carved and designed hardly justifies placing one's head in the excrement!

Many Christians have got putty heads and flint-stony hearts. And in so living we've reversed the order: we ought to be those who have the sharpest, most sensible, thoughtful minds while at the same time cultivating the most passionate, compassionate, artistic and creative emotions. As Martin Luther King said in his book *Strength to Love*, we need tough minds and tender hearts. It's no use looking at a work of painful or truthful art and saying, 'I can't see Jesus or the Holy Spirit in that, so what's it got to do with me?' It's no use listening to a piece of music and saying, 'I can't hear the praises of God in that, so what's it got to do with me?' We need to grow up and respond to art with will, emotions, and intelligence and so hear God's voice speaking to us through it. We need to turn down the volume of our charismatic worship and hear the painful voices of artists like the black writers of the Southern US, or the anguished poets and painters of Central America, who have poured into their work such raging indignation and anger that some of the writings have far greater authenticity and believability than a whole library full of Christian teaching books, than a whole songbook full of Christian choruses. Instead of reacting against art we might condemn as 'unChristian', we should be listening to the message it is screaming at us—and give an intelligent and compassionate response!

In the end, artistic expression and faith are inseparable. We call God the Creator, so all true human artistic endeavour in some way mirrors the creativity of God and in turn gives him glory. When we understand the pain of artists like Bob Dylan, Van Gogh, Dylan Thomas and so many others, we are just beginning to feel the heart of the twentieth century's sense of lostness. The Holy Spirit in his wisdom inspired Paul to recognize that on Mars Hill, and to begin his preaching with Athenian art. (Woody Allen is no preacher, but he knows he can say nothing through his films if he isn't honest about his culture.) This is what makes art so important to the church. This is a post-Christian era, and we have to know the language and the imagery of our age. The old language of hymnbooks and traditional evangelical preaching (though they do have their place) is no longer enough. Communicating in the vernacular has historically been associated with times of renewal in the Church and successful communication to the world.

If we read the Scriptures properly, we soon see that they call us back as much to healing and wholeness in the arts as to healing and wholeness in our sexuality, economics, politics and race relations. If we reject art, we will in the end, because of the power of art, eliminate a major source of understanding our culture and communicating with our age. The danger, then, will be that (like the Jews who left God and worshipped at the feet of the Golden Calf and at the altars of Baal) we will miss God's truth in the art we already have and give our honour instead to the kind of art which twists truth, avoids pain, and celebrates nothing but itself. Just because art does not bear God's name and sign does not mean—will never mean—that God cannot use it. In this analgesic society, art can be a part of our wholeness, a part of God's work in our salvation.

When I was in Adelaide some years ago, there was an arts festival in Elder Park where they had a work of art by a famous Australian sculptor. It was entitled 'The Seven Ages of Man'. It started off with a very large woman very late in pregnancy, whose genitals were somewhat exaggerated to make the point about the pregnancy and the imminent expectation of the arrival of the baby. It traced through the growth from childhood to adulthood, the schoolboy playing sport, the business man with the attaché case, right the way through to the final seventh stage—death. And by the time you'd been right through the whole display and reached the death sculpture, you almost felt relieved. Because what was expressed in each segment of the sculpture display was humanity always at the end of someone else's string. In other words it was a deterministic picture of 'You have no freedom. Life is always under bondage to some other force beyond yourself.'

It was horribly depressing, a wonderful work of art, but terribly disillusioning.

In response to the artwork, some conservative Christians—some right-wing representatives of Jesus in Adelaide—were aghast. They wrote articles about the obscenity, 'This is the people's park. How come we have obscenity in the people's park? The woman in the first piece of sculpture was nude.' They went on and on—it was just unbelievable (especially considering the display was not in the open, but behind hessian walls). I was in the middle of a major outreach program at that time in Adelaide where we spoke to virtually every senior class of students in that city of one million people.

Some people asked me what I thought about it. I said, 'I think people who are reacting like that are crazy. Do you know what I'd do?' I'd been to see it and knew what it was. I said, 'I'd get my hottest, cynical mates, go and have a drink with them in the refectory at the Uni. and say, "Listen you guys, come on in town and let's have a look at this art display. It's a ripper!" And then I'd go in with them and I'd say, "Well, that is the greatest presentation of your religious worldview I've ever seen. I think it's magnificent. In a world where there is no God, that's the way it is! And that has got to be one of the most powerful, honest, full of integrity, emotional statements of the reality you say you believe in." '

According to the Bible we need to be born again (John 3:3–8). 'Born again' Christians love to quote the verse at everybody, yet they don't quote the whole passage. It says, 'Except a person be born again, he or she cannot see the Kingdom of Heaven.' The Kingdom of Heaven is not up there. Not like the little tracts you typically get in evangelistic meetings. Jesus said, 'The Kingdom of God is in the midst of you.' Which means whatever he wants to do, he wants to do in us NOW, even though it'll continue up there. He wants the world different NOW! But the passage continues, 'The wind blows where it wants to. You can hear it; you know it's around but you never know where it's coming from or where it's going. So is everyone who is born of the Spirit.' Now I cannot think of a more predictable, fixed in concrete, group of people than the conservative Christians who most talk about the new birth. But the words of Jesus, who invented the idea, show that people who are truly 'born again' know what it is to move with the Spirit. They are not simply locked in to classic art forms in theology or cartesian logic or anything else. The hope is that God's will gives Christians, as individuals and in groups, the kind of belief system, the kind of knowledge of God that makes them delighted to be living; to celebrate every art form; to enjoy dance, laughter, humour, even irony and cynicism; all those different aspects of the cleverness of the human mind. Yet we must be clear enough about what we believe to be something of a solid rock in the midst of an artistic world which according to two great intellectuals I've read recently, is itself on the edge of self-destruction because it has lost any foundation and has become almost intellectually suicidal. An honest look at the horror of human behaviour and human potential in the negative without grace, faith, hope and love is an awesomely depressing experience.

Christians need to become a people whose artistic mates might feel they're loved, not under constant surveillance; might feel that Jesus expresses love and acceptance and openness. We need to become such a people that the strongest apostolic minds in a community might not look for obscenity, but rather look for a reason behind everything that is done—so that we, like Paul on Mars Hill, might be able to look at the works of art, even if they express a world that is totally different from what we believe, and say, 'I can see underneath it all that there is something happening. You're really very religious. Let's talk about what you're feeling and where you're coming from and let's see if we can find a common point in the stunning revelation of Jesus, in the midst of the pain, the uncertainty and the confusion.'

9

The God Who Meets Us
Where We Are

Just because Christ calls us to face pain and to walk with
him into it does not mean we are left comfortless in it. In
our music, our art, our politics, economics and race relations—wherever we are—Christ meets us. He is the
Word become flesh, and he still dwells among us. That is
what salvation means—wholeness offered to us in our
humanity, not in an escape from its pain. It is a radical
kind of salvation, one that cannot take place except in
total abandonment to the only Person in the universe who
can pay the price of unconditional love and forgiveness.

The Emmaus road

If we surrender our lives to Jesus, reading and devouring
the gospels and seeing their application in everyday life,
then our eyes will be opened; we will not be content with
theology alone, because we will know from experience that
faith without action and application is dead. We will
discover that the gospel is about relationships, not rules.
We will look less for the heaven to come, and more for the
kingdom of heaven that is already in our midst, right here
and now, among the suffering of the world:

> Once, having been asked by the Pharisees when the king-
> dom of God would come, Jesus replied, 'The kingdom of
> God does not come with your careful observation, nor will

people say, "Here it is," or "There it is," because the kingdom of God is in the midst of you.' Then he said to his disciples, 'The time is coming when you will long to see one of the days of the Son of Man, but you will not see it. Men will tell you, "There he is!" or "Here he is!" Do not go running after them. For the Son of Man in his day will be like lightning.... But first he must suffer many things and be rejected by this generation...'

(Luke 17:20–25).

When we thunder out the words 'your kingdom come', we are putting our hand in Jesus' hand. We are saying that however it is in heaven is how we want the earth to be. We are discovering that we can love our enemies rather than hate them. We are seeing the brokenness in the world around us and in ourselves, and we are committing that brokenness to the broken, wounded Jesus, who will heal us. As T.S. Eliot wrote,

> The wounded surgeon plies the steel
> That questions the distempered part;
> Beneath the bleeding hands we feel
> The sharp compassion of the healer's art.
>
> (*Four Quartets*, Faber & Faber)

God is at work in the world, here and now. We don't have to go out looking for signs of his work; they're all around us. He goes ahead of us into every place where we will go, preparing the way for us with his grace. Even before we acknowledged him in our lives, he was pouring out that grace and opening the path to our wholeness. Not only that, but like the father of the prodigal son in Jesus' story, he is running towards us with his arms open wide in welcome and love. His work of saving the world goes on whether we co-operate or not! For every Hitler there is a Mother Teresa. For every southern redneck there is a Martin Luther King—maybe not as obvious or charismatic—but *there*, in a local black or white church down-town.

He was there on the road to Emmaus when two of his friends, missing him and full of doubts about what had been happening in Jerusalem, debated in anguish about the crucifixion and the supposed end to their dreams of a liberated Israel. They longed for him but did not recognise him until he broke the bread; then they remembered his words in the Upper Room: 'This is my body given for you; do this in remembrance of me' (Luke 22:19).

He is there now—where you are—even when we try to compartmentalise our lives and set up one little box for silicon chips, one for picnics with the kids, one for appoint-ments with teachers or dentists, and another for God. But he defies our little boxes!

He is there at whatever point on the journey we are travelling, for we can never stand still in relation to God: either we are moving towards him, or we are moving away from him—though he is with us in either case! (If any-thing, he is nearer to us when we sin and suffer for our sins, because the more sin there is, the more he pours out his love and grace.) Our relationship to him will never be static, for his Spirit is never static; he is a God on the move. He offers us free entry into his gospel feast (see Jesus' story of the man who gave a banquet, in Luke 14:15–24) though this doesn't mean cheap grace; it means transformation for us, a willingness to move with the moving God on our own Emmaus roads: to see him in the bread that is broken, and trust ourselves to him.

The Gethsemane Garden

> Where could I go to escape from you?
> Where could I get away from your presence?
> If I went up to heaven, you would be there;
> If I lay down in the world of the dead, you would be there.
> (Psalm 139:7–8, Good News Bible)

In Victorian days, sad-eyed children stitched samplers reminding them that God was always near. For them, because of the way the Scriptures were then interpreted, this was a frightening rather than a comforting thought. But to the psalmist, the fact that God is always near brings him relief and renewal. 'Between us and God,' it has been said, 'there is no between.' The psalmist knew that even if he went as far away from God as he could, into the depths of hell, God would still be with him.

How reassuring this is. It means that God's grace is so boundless that when we fail as believers he still loves us. He goes on loving us when we sin, even if we go back time and again to the same sin. He wants to free us from the guilt that makes us feel condemned, holding out forgiveness and renewal to us each time, and so liberating us. If we have a different picture of God's love, then we're tragically bound in slavery to an anthropomorphic god who loves conditionally, withdrawing love (as a human being might do) whenever we reject him, or whenever we fail his moral laws (as of course we all do, all the time!).

In answer to this false view of God, the Scriptures remind us of how close he comes to us in pain and brokenness: 'A broken and contrite heart, O God, you will not despise' (Psalm 51:17). As Jesus was a man of sorrows, acquainted with grief, so we who travel with him on the paths to Emmaus and Gethsemane will, in spite of our sin and pain, know him to be very near. We can be free of the false teaching which claims that the minute we hit a hard time God pulls away from us. We can be free of the twisted theology that asks, the minute something goes wrong in our lives, 'What sin have I committed that God is punishing me with this?' God just doesn't work that way!

This means, necessarily, that we are not exempt when we walk with Jesus from having to rub shoulders with the broken world. He offers no protection or insurance policy in that sense. He can keep us courageous in a world of cowardice; he can keep us loving and generous in a world of selfishness; but we will still share with him the pain of Gethsemane, the pain he knew as he looked at the crowds and felt his intestines knotting with the distress of real, deep compassion (Matthew 9:36).

The prodigal son's road home

The story of the lost son (Luke 15:11–32) is so familiar that it seems to many of us to have lost its edge. We need to try to see it freshly if we're to realise how it affects us. To the Jews who heard it straight from Jesus' mouth, it was a scandalous tale of family disloyalty rewarded by love; disloyalty to Judaism rewarded by reconciliation.

Here's this young man living on his father's farm in the country. The place is a bit of a bore: no nightlife, and too many cows to milk at dawn. Dad's getting crusty in his old age, but he's still on the ball enough to organize and engage the young man all day long in farm duties. 'Do this. Do that!' and the young man is sick of everything. Soon the son can stand it no longer and asks to have his share of the family fortune.

Perhaps all this sounds harmless enough to us, but in Jesus' day, in the Middle East, that was an unthinkable request; no other literature recounts that a son asked his father for his share of the property and wealth prior to his death. It would have been tantamount to saying to the father, 'Drop dead, old man, so I can get my fortune!' So there's the first disloyalty, but there is more.

So dad grants the son his request and divides the farm. Off goes the son from Judea, bright-eyed and bushy-tailed, full of plans and dreams that soon come crashing down around his ears in the equivalent of casinos and nightclubs of a neighbouring country, where no one acknowledges his Jewish God. He falls on hard times and gets a job farming pigs. (Not only a non-kosher country, but very definitely non-kosher pigs!) 'Hey, I'm an idiot,' he thinks at last. 'Instead of mucking out these obscene pigsties I could be feeding on the best food my father's table offers. What am I waiting for?'

And in spite of everything, his father not only welcomes him back, but runs to meet him on the road home! He is a father not content with doing self-indulgent, cosy things for his child; rather, he is a father willing to make costly sacrifices. This is not to deny the fact that our wrongdoing and wrong attitudes destroy relationships with God and our fellow humans. 'It is your sins that separate you from God,' Isaiah reminds us (Isaiah 59:2).

In the fractured homes of the twentieth century, many people do not experience the love of God as a heavenly Father—because they haven't even known the love of any earthly father. It's helpful for them, especially, but in fact for all of us, to think of God as both Father and Mother. Men and women are, after all, both made in the image of God; and since God transcends gender, we need to understand that God's personality is both male and female in its expression. Like the traditional, good father he is strong for us, protecting, providing and forgiving. Like a mother she is gentle for us, nurturing, brooding, storing up in her heart the wonder of loving parenthood, as Mary did when she pondered the wonder of Jesus' birth.

God is not simply our divine Father; God is our divine Parent. Like the father of the prodigal son in Jesus' story, God welcomes us home with eager arms, no matter what. Our brothers and sisters may give up on us, but God doesn't. Our teachers and employers may write terminally bad reports on us, but God doesn't. Our pastors and preachers may dismiss us because we've failed, but God is not (praise be!) like such preachers. God never behaves like imperfect earthly parents and leaders; he (she) is different: 'Though my father and mother forsake me, the Lord will receive me' (Psalm 27:10). God is also described as a faithful spouse in such prophesies as Hosea, but it is doubtful if a greater image of parental care is to be found than in Hosea 11:1–4.

False views of salvation

Me, me, me!
God's desire to heal and redeem the world is not confined, much as we sometimes like to think, to nicely scrubbed Sunday best white suburban Western people; nor is it confined to any individuals. God is interested in salvation not in the singular, not in isolation, but in the plural—in community. God's plans are far bigger than me; he wants to redeem all creation, and we're just a part of his plan! We say we believe he is the Lord of all, but do we? Do we really believe he is Lord of and watching over all the world's pain, laughter, sadness, and struggle? Or have we instead turned God into a cosmic bellboy, a genie at our beck and call?

Salvation can't be comprehended in four neat little 'spiritual laws'; instead it means that God wants to deliver us from every force, every power that in any way dehumanises and destroys his universe. Nor can salvation be comprehended in a list of private moral laws (see Job 31) but includes also an understanding of and response to the needs of the environment, before our land 'cries out against [us] and all its furrows are wet with tears' (Job 31:38). Salvation is a cosmic concern—and the Bible said so, long before the New Agers! It is nonsense to talk in an idolatrous way exclusively about 'my personal relationship with Jesus' when we speak of salvation (as if modern Western individualism were the only way to read the Scriptures); for God's gospel cries out for total healing— no blight, no brokenness, no tears, no hunger, no disease—in the entire cosmos.

If we truly understand God as our heavenly parent, perhaps we'll better understand how God feels about our treatment of his gifts to us. Think of it: the Parent gives his/her children a blue and green planet of cloud, land and water, plants and animals, birds and fish...and we set about destroying it as systematically and greedily as we can. It's as if we are teenagers who, having received beautiful birthday presents from our parents, take the family car and drive it back and forth over them until they are all crushed. In our blind self-indulgence, we pit financial prosperity against the value of species dying daily, species that contribute in small, hidden, yet important ways to the well-being of the whole world. We have only to remember President Bush's refusal to sign the bio-diversity convention at the Rio summit in 1992 to see in microcosm the greed of the entire West! Thank God there are some Christian voices of the calibre of Peter Garrett of 'Midnight Oil' and Bruce Cockburn in the rock music world whose art is committed to justice and environmental renewal. We prefer to hop into our fuel-guzzling and carbon-producing cars to drive half a mile for a pint of milk in a plastic bottle that will not decompose for over a million years than to make a few small changes that may help God in his work of redeeming the planet.

Our greedy, selfish, and limited understanding of salvation stems from today's individualism. Like the prodigal son, we want to go off and do our own thing, regardless of what pain we inflict on the world around us. We have turned the gospel from the question 'What can I contribute? How can I love others?' to 'How can I get happy?' But we need each other; we need families, friends, communities, neighbours, fellowship and togetherness—and an environment which reflects the creative diversity of God almighty.

There's no such thing as purely private salvation; we simply can't be saved in a vacuum. Even modern physics teaches us that. (The chaos theory explains that when a butterfly lifts its wings on one side of the cosmos, the 'ripple' effects from that miniscule movement spill out into the entire universe, and nothing is ever the same again!) We have cheapened the gospel, reducing it to the purely personal: 'I'm OK as long as I feel good, as long as I feel a sense of worth because of what I've achieved or how I look.' Martin Luther King reminds us that,

> All men (and women) are interdependent. Every nation is an heir of a vast treasury of ideas and labour to which both the living and the dead of all nations have contributed. Whether we realize it or not, each of us lives eternally 'in the red'. We are everlasting debtors to known and unknown men and women. When we arise in the morning, we go into the bathroom where we reach for a sponge which is provided for us by a Pacific islander. We reach for soap that is created for us by a European. Then at the table we drink coffee which is provided for us by a South American, or tea by a Chinese, or cocoa by a West African. Before we leave for our jobs we are already beholden to more than half of the world.
>
> (*The Words of Martin Luther King*, Selected by Coretta Scott King, Collins FOUNT PAPERBACKS)

Like the legendary character Narcissus, we have fallen in love with the reflection of ourselves and missed the true source in whose image we have been made: the Creator himself.

In so doing we have also missed the wonder, delight and scintillating liveliness we can find in him—the endless possibilities he wants to open to us. In so doing we end up swallowing the analgesics and pep pills of a 'Christian' slogan society that feeds on a few nice choruses, and a few items of Jesus paraphenalia. We take the cola advert that proclaims 'Things go better with Coke' and insert 'Jesus' for the word 'Coke'. We sing 'Amazing grace, how sweet the sound that saved a wretch like me', but we don't feel wretched at all—only slightly smug about having joined a nice little club, in this case ecclesiastical. We stop seeing that faith means radical transformation relevant to the hurts of the world. We don't realise that the 'swine' we are not supposed to throw our 'pearls' in front of aren't those supposedly unfit to hear the gospel…but are those who think they're more than fit to hear it: the holy people. (Sometimes, those self-righteous people include us!)

Rules, not relationships?

Just as we often privatise salvation, so we foolishly privatise sin. We think of it in terms of whether we've masturbated, or read pornographic magazines, or missed a prayer meeting. We strain at those 'gnats' and swallow the 'camels' of injustice and lack of mercy. We cry, 'Ah, but I've been born again,' and then we condone the bombing of Argentine ships, Libyan cities, or Iraqi women and children.

We are forgetting Jesus' story of those who will enter his kingdom:

> I was hungry and you gave me something to eat. I was thirsty and you gave me something to drink, I was a stranger and you invited me in, I needed clothes and you clothed me, I was sick and you looked after me, I was in prison and you came to visit me.
>
> (Matthew 25:35–36)

We would sometimes rather legislate than communicate, excommunicate rather than befriend, despise rather than reconcile. We would rather attend Bible studies on the Book of Amos than ask questions of our local politicians about the way the poor are treated by our government and—indirectly—by ourselves. Like the Pharisees Jesus was attacking in this part of Matthew's gospel, we neglect the things that really count if the kingdom is to come on earth. We fuss about keeping Sunday special not because (if we're honest) we want to spend more of Sunday in worship with our families, but because the noise of increased traffic, commerce and sport shatter the comfortable peace of our lazy Sunday afternoons on the patio. We preach Christian stewardship or tithing not because we want to give more time and money to the poor, but because we want to preserve what we've got and renovate the sanctuary. I came across an astonishing statement from the early church:

> Do you really wish to pay homage to Christ's body? Then do not neglect him when he is naked. At the same time that you honor him here [in church] with hangings made of silk, do not ignore him outside when he perishes from cold and nakedness. For the One who said 'This is my body'...also said 'When I was hungry you gave me nothing to eat.'...For is there any point in his table being laden with golden cups while he himself is perishing from hunger? First fill him when he is hungry and then set his table with lavish ornaments. Are you making a golden cup for him at the very moment when you refuse to give him a cup of cold water? Do you decorate his table with cloths flecked with gold, while at the same time you neglect to give him what is necessary for him to cover himself?...I'm saying all this not to forbid your gifts of munificence, but to admonish you to perform those other duties at the same time, or rather before, you do these. No one was ever condemned for neglecting to be munificent: for the neglect of others hell itself is threatened, as well as unquenchable fire.... The conclusion is: Don't neglect your brother in his distress while you decorate his house. Your brother is more truly his temple than any church building.
>
> (St John Chrysostom, quoted in *The Faith that does Justice*. Edited by John C. Haughey, PAULIST PRESS)

Mindlessness

Many people when they first confess faith in Jesus begin to wonder, because of shoddy teaching in the church, whether they are supposed to switch off their minds and rely entirely on the promptings of the Holy Spirit; on whether something 'seems' or 'feels' right. Of course we are to rely on the promptings of the Spirit, and of course we are to search the Scriptures and our own experience to know the course of action God would have us take. But we certainly aren't intended to switch off our God-given intelligence. God is about the business of redeeming our attitudes and our thinking processes as much as our souls. It is nonsense to suppose otherwise; unlike animals we are not limited to response based on instinct; we're given sanctified common sense!

All too easily we satisfy ourselves with the pap of contemporary video and rock and roll material. All too easily we subside into our padded armchairs before the television and soak up the mindless drivel that jitters and bleats at us from the box. All too easily we slide into the somnolent comfort of charismatic choruses. We let them wash over us without thinking of words or implications. We let the ecstatic experience magnify while the grasp of truth diminishes. We let shallow and dangerous thinking invade us without asking questions or putting up any resistance. The seeds of destructive and twisted thinking take root in us, and we don't even know they've fallen into our 'soul'! We are being naive if we think we can remain neutral before this tide of mindlessness.

Alternatively, but equally destructively, we reject feelings altogether and function as if we were all brain and no heart; all cerebrum and no celebration. We love the theological frameworks, but we hate the fireworks they threaten to light under our cosy lives. Unlike Paul when he was addressing the Athenians on Mars Hill and drawing thoughtfully from contemporary sculpture and poetry in his reasoning, we either neglect our minds or retreat so far into them that we're completely out of touch with the heart-woundedness and the intensity of the world's alienation. Neither path is productive; neither will bring us closer to the kingdom of God which is already in the midst of us demanding our committed response.

There are many 'seed-sowers' in our world, broadcasting to us (as seed-sowers did in biblical times) handfuls of seeds that contain weed-seeds as well as fruit-bearing seeds. Young people resent being told by their parents not to listen to or watch certain things, but do older people impose similar restrictions on themselves? If not, why not? Are we content to swallow all the lies, trivialities, and fantasies? Or do we need to exercise some discriminations?

I once met a man in Melbourne who had become more obsessed as a Christian with demons than with the Person and work of Jesus. Every time he came to our centre he talked about the help the Holy Spirit had given him in throwing demons out of people and places. It so happened that across the road from our centre was a manufacturer called Fibre Makers; they made women's underwear by a process that apparently involved sulphur. On days when production was in full swing and the wind was blowing the wrong way, the acrid smell of sulphur permeated the centre.

One day when he'd been coming to the centre for a while he suddenly began to mutter the name of Beelzebub. I was dazed and just stared blankly at him. 'Beelzebub! Beelzebub!' he repeated, then 'Sulphur! Sulphur comes from hell, and wherever Beelzebub is, you can smell sulphur. I can always tell when he's around. We'd better call a meeting, John, and cast him out of this place. It's definitely Beelzebub.' He was a deeply committed brother but he simply made no sense at all. Faith had become almost mindless superstition.

On another occasion a former shop floor steward came into the centre to talk with us. 'I've got to get out of the union,' he said. 'Why?' I asked him. 'There's a verse in the Bible that says you can't be in a trade union,' he insisted, and showed me 1 Timothy 3:3 in his King James Version: 'Not given to wine, *no striker*, not greedy of filthy lucre; but patient, not a brawler, not covetous.' Then he explained that a 'wonderful' preacher had just been to his church and had preached on the words 'no striker'. Unionists go on strike, he said, so the Bible condemns union membership! Thinking of the early days of the British trade union movement, which had based its championing of exploited workers on biblical principles, I was surprised at the reaction of both men and turned up the same verse in the NIV: 'Not given to drunkenness, not violent but gentle, not quarrelsome, not a lover of money.' Here was a simple matter of an archaic translation, one that had been applied slavishly to the detriment of this man's career.

Do we need intelligence in our faith? The answer is obvious. And we need that intelligence not just outside the church, but within it. It's time we realised that living spiritually, living in a relationship with God, does not mean living stupidly. C. S. Lewis said that in some ways faith reminded him of the sun, not because we look at the sun, but because in the light of the sun everything else can be seen more clearly. And so it is that real faith, intelligent faith, makes sense of many things for us. But if our 'faith' mystifies, clouds and confuses everything, and if it shuts down the most stunning part of our anatomy, the brain, then it's a long way from the real faith Jesus taught and wanted us to espouse.

In fact we forget that the term 'heart', biblically speaking, is an all-embracing term including the faculties of mind, emotions and will. Jesus' teaching was directed at minds as well as hearts. The Scriptures aren't full of airy-fairy notions and warm feelings; they're hard-headed and present us with debates about economics, racism, peace, human guilt, sexuality, justice and oppression, the rights of women—virtually everything modern humanity needs to learn about how to live. When we get bogged down in petty arguments and narrow applications of verses out of context or badly translated, we have ceased to think. And we have ceased to live in real faith.

True views of salvation

If we can safely reject egotism, legalism and mindlessness as inadequate ways of understanding our faith, how then are we to understand salvation? No doubt whole books could be written in answer to this question, but here are at least three valid views of salvation that will help us walk the path of faith on which Jesus is both beside and ahead of us.

First, we can be sure that God desires and loves his creation as much and far more than any one of us desires and loves any other person. We can also be confident of his ability to fill the aching void within us. And, along the way, like the two men walking to Emmaus, not only will we want to ask questions, but we can be certain that God will prompt us to do so. Following these views of salvation will keep us free from the traps of greedy individualism, over-emphasis on rules, and unthinking words and actions.

Secondly, we are saved *for* something, not just *from* something. When we talk about knowing Jesus personally and having been saved by him, we often do so at the expense of others. We are arrogant, exclusive and unloving, putting ourselves ahead of others and ahead of the environment God has given us. Such a lack of mercy and compassion is the very opposite of a loving God, whose longing is that we change, that we cross the gulf between ourselves and others, and that we express his passion for the underdogs who have no voice but Christ's. St Paul states that the death of Christ for all challenges all the 'walls of partition' we erect in hostility towards others.

Thirdly, we are declared to be a new creation. A new identity—a love-centred rather than ego-centred identity—is ours in Christ. When we do choose the Christian faith we have made a scary choice. Our identities are about to be remade in a radical way. We have to give up our idea that what we do—at work, school, home, in church, in bed—defines who we are; we discover that we are more than the sum total of what we do. We find that, far from being the chance product of chemical reactions in a meaningless universe, we are created in God's image for a unique and fantastic destiny—something that has little to do with our narrow understanding of self-worth (real self-worth only comes when there is nothing between us, God and our fellow-humans). We have to commit ourselves to walking the road with Jesus to discover what that destiny is, what that unique reflection of God's image means for us—but also what it means for the world. This is what salvation means.

When God created the world, and before sin entered it, he looked at it and said, 'It's a bobbydazzler! It's so good!' But now that sin has entered in and spoiled everything, God is filled with desire to recreate the world: to recreate forests we have felled for paper and timber; to recreate relationships we have broken in our haste to scramble into something 'better'. He longs, in fact, to recreate the love, caring and wholeness that was there in the beginning. He desires to change human beings radically, yes; but then he expects us to take part in recreating the rest of his creation. In *Smash Hits*, Peter Garrett stated, 'In the years to come, it will seem incredible that we treated Earth as a garbage tip and lived as though there was no tomorrow. This fragile planet is a miracle, and we're destroying it' ('Rebels with a Cause', in *Smash Hits*, 17 October, 1990). In fact St Paul pictures 'the entire creation groaning and longing for a liberation' in which the sons and daughters of God are mysteriously engaged.

What will this involve? We are called to build bridges across the gulf between God and others. Right from the days of Jesus' ministry on earth this has been so. When Jesus healed people, he did not call them out of their confused and hurting lives only to enter monastic communities or go alone on itinerant preaching tours (though these are worthy pursuits). Those he called were always either sent back into their own communities or commissioned for work in teams with other believers. He encouraged them to follow his own example and befriend those outcast in society: in his day the lepers, tax collectors, prostitutes and publicans; in our day those with the HIV virus, outlaw motorcyclists and teenage gangs, victims of crime, prison inmates, pregnant teenagers and kerb crawlers, drug addicts and the homeless—anyone despised or neglected by society who must be included in the world 'God so loved' (John 3:16, 17).

Jesus never said to sinners, the poor and needy, 'Come all of you into church to hear the gospel.' Instead he told us to carry the gospel to every corner of the earth! This means we have to abandon our churchy language and communicate with people (as Jesus does with us) exactly where they are and in terms they understand. We don't start with the attitude: 'Here I am, pal, and God sent me to save you, you scum! Here's my Bible, and I'm going to whack you with it because I've got myself together, and you're a mess until you accept Jesus as your personal Saviour as I did.' Rather, we begin from a place of humility, seeing in others a reflection of God's particular image in them, God's longing for them; and seeing ourselves only as his messengers, working relationally from day to day with them, perhaps not even directly mentioning the name of Jesus for a long time, until we have earned their trust, until they have begun asking questions, and until they have seen our love in action. This is a costly, difficult way to witness to our faith, but it is the only way that will bring true salvation to most people.

I've found that out for myself many times, particularly once in Cardiff, where I had gone for a conference and Rubber Hits the Road concert at a Baptist church just outside the city. Things had gone wrong; my wife and I had had a bad day and I was feeling sorry for myself.

Then I heard the Spirit's gentle prompting: 'You think you feel rotten, Smithie? Why not take yourself down to the nearest pub and find out who really feels unhappy?'— and with good reason.

Mentally and spiritually shaking myself, I went off rather reluctantly. I soon found myself in a smoke-filled working-class bar where men were knocking down the alcohol as if there were no tomorrow, playing snooker, and socializing in an alcoholic haze. They picked up my Aussie accent immediately and wanted to know with a lot of teasing why I hadn't got a crocodile slung over my shoulder and corks hanging round my hat. Then one man befriended me, welcoming me in some ways more warmly than I had been welcomed in many churches. We talked and talked about our families, and he told me that after fathering eight children he was just going through his second divorce. His face was filled with pain as he said, 'If only someone could tell me what life's all about and what it means, I could survive this tragedy.'

I was shattered and humbled. It crossed my mind that except for the prompting of the Spirit to me that evening, this man might have sat in the pub for a solid ten years before another professed 'spiritual' person crossed his path. We could have run our Christian concerns and missions only yards across the street for years on end, and this man would never have heard the gospel because the church wasn't coming out to him. I felt ashamed that we weren't bringing our music to the pub but keeping it in the relative safety of the church.

We call ourselves Christ's body. This means that we are his hands and feet, arms, eyes, ears, and voice in the world. Knowing his salvation, then, we must not only share it with our mouths but live it in lives of mercy, love, and care for the needy. The Old Testament prophets' vision of the future was not of a warm, happy paradise but of a world which was fair; where people can live in safety;

where there will be enough water for dry lands and dry mouths; where there will be no more exploitation and violence.

Being Christ's body in the world means, for example, that men cannot any longer see women (as did the Pharisees) as sex objects, servants in the home, and slaves. It means that we must forgive those who hurt us—emotionally, financially, physically; that we must love our enemies. It means that parents have to stop seeing their children as extensions of their own egos and desires and begin to see them instead as God's children made in his image to accomplish his particular purposes for humanity and God, not theirs alone. It means that judges and barristers can no longer continue finding people guilty just because the system has made them so poor they can't pay bills, let alone legal costs; that wealth cannot and should not guarantee favourable verdicts while poverty guarantees conviction, guilt or no guilt. It means that social workers and teachers cannot set themselves above the people with whom they work, but must humbly see them as fellow children of God, people from whom they too can learn something. It means that publishers and publishing conventions should not ask for funds from the third world for publishing some of its treasures in the West, while at the same time offering no expertise to third-world publishers to do their own publishing and promoting, dealing indigenously and interdependently rather than dependently with their social and political dilemmas.

Being Christ's body in the world means not grabbing for all the fun and all the goods we can get, stuffing ourselves intellectually, commercially and physically, and then saying we have no money to give to deprived children or medical research. It means hearing the cry of anguish from drug addicts, alcohol addicts, food and exercise addicts—even music addicts—and responding to it. It means writing letters to Amnesty International on behalf of those tortured and imprisoned in brutal circumstances in other countries—or even in our own. It means loving the people no one else has the courage to love—the people on the edge: pregnant teenagers; indigenous people; gypsies; those with senile dementia; the illiterate; the widowed, orphaned, and lonely; the mentally disturbed; those who have been raped or abused; divorcees...

Being Christ's body in the world means humbling ourselves enough to give up our perspective of privilege, power and possession and then to ask those at the bottom of society's heap to help us see the world as they see it— from the underbelly—and so work to change it.

And if we do some of these things, we will enter the kingdom St Paul describes in Romans chapters 12–14: the kingdom of righteousness—a righteousness that means social, political, emotional, relational, and spiritual wholeness. *Then* we will know what salvation is!

God's ability to fill the void

God desires the full salvation of all his creation. We need never doubt it. Neither need we doubt his ability, once we acknowledge our emptiness, to fill the aching void in creation. As he filled it in the first days of the Creation, so he goes on filling it in his work of re-creation. As Jesus said, we cannot live by bread alone; there is more to us, more to the cosmos, than flesh and blood, minerals and gases. While the rest of the cosmos may not know its need of God, yet still praises him (Psalm 19), human beings have in their hearts something that cries out for a definitive word about our identity, our aspirations, our meaning. The cross of Christ is not a sign of failure and finality, but of God's certainty of our worth, his hope for our new beginnings and his identification with our powerlessness. He alone can fill the aching emptiness of the world's heart.

More than twenty questions

We don't travel far with Jesus without asking questions; an absence of questioning probably indicates that we are bordering on the kind of mindlessness I described before. Paul reminds us of this in his letter to the Romans:

> Therefore, I urge you, brothers, in view of God's mercy, to offer your bodies as living sacrifices, holy and pleasing to God—this is your spiritual act of worship. Do not conform any longer to the pattern of this world, but be transformed *by the renewing of your mind.*
>
> (Romans 12:1–2)

Since our brains are part of our bodies, and since we want to worship God with our lives, we need to engage our minds as well as our emotions. We aren't going to change patterns of destruction to the environment, patterns of destruction in families and politics, unless we use our brains and raise questions about what we see and hear.

We need to be intelligent about our faith, our friendships, and our finances. We need to stop conveying the impression that we have our lives and our thinking all sewn up, and that no one can teach us anything. We have to stop running away from the people on the edges of society just because their nearness makes us so full of puzzlement and disturbing questions. Then, as part of our coming into wholeness, shalom, salvation, we shall know at least some of the answers to the huge questions of where we belong, why we're here, and who we are. We must face the pain in our lives because pain itself will guide us into the questions that are burning holes in our lives.

We will not know all the answers right away, for some of them will remain hidden until we meet Christ face to face, but we will certainly know the boundless love, forgiveness and freedom of God's grace.

Lastly, the process of asking questions will require us as

Westerners to rediscover our 'tribal' roots. Communication, commitment, compassion are not the prerogative of the isolated ego but of community. Unless we take our place in a *communion* of the concerned and committed we will swiftly burn out at the enormity and apparent endlessness of the task before us.

10

Loose Ends

In an excellent book of weekly 'meditations and prayers for busy people', my long-term friend Rowland Croucher has included a chapter entitled 'Life's loose ends'. This theme is one which we need to truly grapple with if we are serious about being on the cutting edge. The following quotes are from this notable chapter.

> Man has an inveterate habit of what I should call a premature tidiness. He is a little previous, strapping up the luggage of his mind before he has everything in, summing up and pronouncing judgment before he has heard all the evidence, dabbing on labels without noting the contents of the parcels. We classify too hurriedly; it saves the bother of tedious discrimination—tares, wheat, sheep, goats, those who are right, those who are wrong.
>
> (A.E. Whitham, *The Pastures of His Presence*, as quoted in *Still Waters, Deep Waters*. Edited by Rowland Croucher [Albatross])

We like to have everything tied up, not because we want the truth, but because we don't want the sheer toughness of having to trust God when the answers aren't in and the labels don't fit the contents in the box. It's not really a good, clean, 'I love God and want the truth' motivation. It's 'please, I don't want to be bugged by too much contradiction, by too much trouble, by too many doubts. I want to walk by sight and not by faith.'

> In recent years the magnificent pinetrees in Kensington Park...have been dying. Experts say there can be little doubt that this is due to the misdirected tidiness of the gardeners, who swept up the old dead pine-needles and left the roots without natural comfort and protection.
>
> (Old newspaper cutting, as quoted in *Still Waters, Deep Waters*)

So the over-tidy garden has killed the magnificent old trees. And you know some of us can only walk with God and only walk in the fellowship of the church, when there are no demands, no conflicts and no struggles. We do to each other what we do to God. If there's a bit of conflict and a bit of struggle between us, we quit and give it up as a bad show because it's got to be so tidy, it's got to be so neat. In the search for neatness we kill the roots of both faith and fellowship.

> Coherency is God's gift; he gives it freely but it can only be received by those who preserve an untidiness of mind. The tidy mind is not the truthful mind; the utterance that leaves no room for doubt or place for question is the fruit of a mind that is full of unwarranted conclusions. To think truly, and to speak and act truthfully...a minister of the Word must deliberately preserve an untidy mind. This untidiness of mind will irritate him; he will often be weary of living in what seems a mental muddle...Generally his respite consists in the realisation that to bear the burden of this muddle is the true way of preserving real knowledge.
>
> (R.E.C. Browne, *The Ministry of the Word*, as quoted in *Still Waters, Deep Waters*)

Last year I was called on to perform the funeral of a dear friend of my daughter Kathy. He was an American in his mid 20's who had helped her immensely when, at 18 years of age, she was alone in Europe. While in Australia, he got caught up in some New Year's Eve revelry and tragically ended up being run over by a truck.

As an ex-Catholic who had become alienated from the church, he had read over one hundred books of every sort trying to find out what life is about. He left behind some journals of his thinking which showed his wonderfully clear, lucid, creative and searching mind that was somehow also as mad as a mad man's breakfast—his thoughts were profound on the one hand yet he had also assimilated some very weird thinking as well.

The mark of modern youth has become two things: either terminal boredom and the inability to search for anything, or else almost the opposite—fanaticism, whether it be about sex, or drugs, or knowledge—as in that melancholic song by The Eagles. There was an element of their 'Take it to the Limit One More Time' mixed up in much of the thinking evidenced in this young man's journal.

In my own search I opened up a devotional book and I read an article entitled 'Life's Loose Ends'. Life is full of loose ends, particularly in our society. Once we had what is called a consensus—there was a body of generally agreed-upon data about relationships, about God. You mightn't have gone to church but you basically agreed that there was someone back up there, and if you went too far over the line, someone was going to smack your fingers in the cosmic tomorrow. There was, at least, some basic agreement within Western culture. Now it's fragmented. It's like a thousand pieces of broken glass reflecting light in different directions. It is as if the mind is fragmented in the search—seeing a glittering bit of light from a broken bit of glass of ideas in this direction, and then another one captures your eye over here, and the light is no longer focussed in a beam of truth, but broken into shattered insights, unrelated to each other, self-contradictory, all over the place. To me this provides a powerful image of

today's new generation. Don't let anyone ever fool you—
this generation needs the voices of those of us getting on a
bit, and of those my parents' age who sometimes have
wonderful insights learned in the university of the hard
knocks of life. Today's generation, believe me, has lost it!
It has so little to offer. As Woody Allen stated in 'Manhattan', we are reduced to an age of people:

> who are constantly creating these real, unnecessary neurotic problems for themselves 'cause it keeps them from
> dealing with more unsolvable, terrifying problems about
> the universe.

Mental breakdown literally becomes for many a chance
to escape the contradictions of living in a broken world.

Life, now, has become for many people—loose ends.
An element of that has always existed, as the following
Bible stories show:

'How long are you going to keep us in suspense? Tell us
the plain truth. Are you the Messiah?' (Luke 7:19). (Come
on Jesus—make it clean, tidy, straight-forward and simple. Are you or aren't you? What we want is a good
fundamentalist response. Give us a three point outline.
Tell us exactly where it lays and we'll go out and we'll put
it all on cable, commercial and public television and on
every radio and publishing organisation and we'll shove it
down every throat all across Europe and America. Please
tell us—are you or aren't you? Let's get it clear. We don't
like this uncertainty, this ambiguity, these little hints that
you give and then leave us to have to work for ourselves to
find out what it really means. We don't like that stuff—
just lay it out. We're bone lazy, mental couch potatoes.)

Or: 'Tell us,' they asked Jesus, 'Are you the one John
said was going to come, or should we expect someone
else?' (Luke 7:20). (Don't taunt us, tease us, provoke us
and challenge us with theological loose ends!)

Or try this story: 'At about the ninth hour, Jesus cried

with a loud voice "My God! My God! Why has thou forsaken me?" ' (Luke 15:34). (Another dreaded loose end! Jesus is God. Jesus talks to God. Jesus the Son plans with God for the redemption of the world. Now he says 'Hey, how come you let me down?' What does that mean? Had he forgotten what he was there for? Do YOU know everything? To what extent did the incarnation, as a voluntary act by God, limit the God-in-the-flesh to less than a full understanding of even what he was doing? We don't like that, do we? That's too much of a loose end.)

Here's another one: 'Now we see only puzzling reflections in a mirror, but then we shall see face to face. My knowledge now is partial, then it will be made whole, like God's knowledge of me' (1 Corinthians 13:12). (But not in this life, baby! How do you live with loose ends?)

And another one: Here's a man (John 9) being healed. The theologians come to him. In fact these were conservative, fundamentalist theologians—the Pharisees. They believed in verbal, total inspiration of the Torah. They believed in morality. They believed in prayer. They believed in fasting and Jesus said they were even evangelistic to the point that they would go from one end of the planet to the other to make one new convert. But they come to a man who doesn't understand all this stuff, but who was blind, met Jesus and now he sees. And they said, 'Come on, this man that healed you, we happen to know he's theologically off the cognitive map. He's not a good man at all. He's a bad influence inside of the Jewish faith.'

And the man replied, 'I don't know if he's a sinner or not. One thing I do know, I was blind and now I see.' (You can talk about political correctness, theological correctness, or anything else you like! But who's gonna deny it, baby? I can see!)

Or what about this story? (Matthew 13:24–30): 'Do you want us to go and pull up the weeds?' they asked Jesus. 'No!' he answered, 'because as you gather the weeds, you might pull up some of the wheat along with them. Let the weeds and the wheat grow together until the harvest.' (The objective seems clear enough; there's the good stuff—there's the bad stuff, let's pull up the bad stuff, get rid of it. But Jesus prefers to leave them with a loose end. He seems to say that the bad stuff's going to have to stick around too, because really, you're not going to be wise enough and precise enough to know which is the bad stuff, which is the good stuff. You're really going to wreck it. That's our task—to decide who goes down and who comes up.)

Or this one? (Matthew 16:12): Jesus said, 'I have yet many things to say to you but you cannot bear them now.' (How frustrating! You're a disciple of Jesus, you want to do exactly what he wants you to do. Parents pull this one on you, don't they?—'What do you really think, Dad?' 'Well, I'm not going to tell you because frankly if I really told you what I think, we would have another row. I'm not going to tell you.' Ever heard that? Ever heard that from your spouse? Jesus did that to his disciples: 'Yeah, there are some other things, there are some other answers. But, sorry, I'm not going to tell you. You couldn't handle it if I gave you the full deal.' That's pretty deflating, isn't it? Loose ends!)

And how many psalms ask questions like 'Oh Lord, how long must I call for your help before you listen and before you save us from violence?'

And I couldn't leave this theme without a word from Job (Job 23:1–5): 'I still rebel and complain against God. How I wish I knew where to find him and knew how to go where he is. I would state my case before him and present all the arguments in my favour. I want to know what he would say and how he would answer me.'

Now, my dear friends, there are two things that have to exist like two loose ends; like shoe laces undone. At the more liberal end of the church, you'll find that many people have no answers for anything. There is nothing one can assert, there is nothing one can believe. The intellectual framework is that you get your theological adrenalin out of constantly raising questions and never having anything answered. In the modern Western world, having no answers is seen as highly intelligent. It means you can say almost anything and look smart. You never commit yourself to anything so nobody can ever prove you're wrong with a future PhD thesis. It's all very self-serving. It's an inverted egotistical world view which underscores a strange dichotomy regarding human beings.

There are many people who, if all the ends are tied up, are going to immediately feel insulted intellectually and spiritually. When religious leaders or others attempt to give simplistic answers, these people will say 'Forget it, pal, that doesn't stretch my mind at all. I want something with intellectual depth.' There are other people who feel far less secure, and need to be given something solid that they can feel confident about and say 'I can believe this. I believe this to be lastingly true.' Now of course it's true that we are all in different stages of pilgrimage, but in the West now, there are multitudes of loose ends, so many things of which we can't make sense and for which we are unable to arrive at simple solutions. Unless you're in a very fundamentalist church, where the preacher simply says, 'This is the interpretation of this passage. This is what you believe in this church,' you're living in a world where there will always be many loose ends, intellectually, socially and personally.

Let us consider, then, some more quotes from *Still Waters, Deep Waters*.

> It is not that we are reduced to struggling through life on a balance of probabilities. Chesterton reminded us that the only virtue of having an open mind is that, like an open mouth, you can close it on something. We come as close to the certainty we crave as we are ever likely to do at the

point of our commitment to Christ, when we can say, 'One thing I know: I was blind and I can see—however dimly,' and trust him for the rest.

(Still Waters, Deep Waters)

Never get things too clear. Religion can't be clear. In this mixed-up life there is always an element of unclearness...If I could understand religion as I understand that two and two make four, it would not be worth understanding. Religion can't be clear if it is worth having. To me, if I can see things through, I get uneasy—I feel it's a fake, I know I have left something out, I've made a mistake.

(Baron von Hugel, in Introduction to
Letters from Baron Friedrick von Hugel to a Niece,
as quoted in *Still Waters, Deep Waters*)

I went to the theatre
With the author of a successful play.
He insisted on explaining everything;
Told me what to watch;
The details of directions,
The errors of the property man,
The foibles of the star.
He anticipated all my surprises
And ruined the evening.
Never Again!

(Christopher Morley, *No Coaching*, as quoted in *Still Waters, Deep Waters*

And to vary Christopher Morley's conclusion, 'The gospel writers, who each knew the greatest author of all, didn't make such a mistake.' They left us with enough loose ends that if we're awake to it, they are saying to us, 'Don't overestimate your capacity to understand, and don't become so technical that you lose the beauty of the art of faith and love.'

But all that seems to make nonsense of the world, all the irrationalities and defeats, the waste, the sheer negation and futility which makes life seem like a tale told by an idiot, are concentrated in the cross of Christ. That was utter, irrational meaninglessness, the apparent denial of any faith in God, any confidence in truth or goodness.

It is no use asking, What sense does it make? The whole point is, surely, that *Jesus made sense of it*, working negativity and non-meaning into the ultimate pattern of God's purpose.

(F.R. Barry, *Asking the Right Questions*,
as quoted in *Still Waters, Deep Waters*)

Job never found an answer to the problem of unmerited suffering. The problem remained insoluble, but in it he met God. That is where man always meets God. That is where man most frequently meets his fellows. For he is so constituted that he needs problems more than solutions. His soul thrives on questions, but grows sickly on answers—especially answers served up by others and, most of all, answers laid down by authority.

(John V. Taylor, *The Go-Between God*,
as quoted in *Still Waters, Deep Waters*)

At the funeral of my daughter Kathy's friend, we sat with a house-full of people with no church background—people with broken marriages, people with their kids on drugs, people with all sorts of problems just pouring out. Why? In the unanswerable question of a 26-year-old's unnecessary and premature death, and the mystery of his wonderful personal diary, we were brought together, pagans and believers. We all started from a common point, that life was too big and its questions too hurtful and too demanding for any of us to survive them alone. So we sought each other in a memorial service, with most of us not even knowing what to do on such an occasion. So they turned to me, asking, 'You're an expert, please tell us what to do.' What could I do? I said, 'I can't make sense of it either, even though I'm the minister here. But I do want to give you one thing I can make sense of, and that's in the book of Isaiah, talking about someone called Jesus: "Surely he has borne our griefs and carried our sorrows." '

It doesn't answer the untidy ends, but it brings light in the midst of the darkness.

When John the Baptist died, Jesus didn't even want to talk to his disciples. He went away. He was distraught—and he prayed to his father in Heaven, alone. Not long before John the Baptist was killed, he went through his own crisis and questioning. And he began to doubt whether Jesus was who he thought he was, so he sent his mates (the few he had left because most of his road crew had gone off to follow Jesus, he didn't even have his roadies, let alone his crowd any more) telling them: 'Ask Jesus: Are you the Messiah or do we look for someone else?' (Matthew 11:3).

He was loose-ended in his thinking, but Jesus' response, I believe, gives us a vital clue as to how to live with complications, contradictions, insufficient details—loose ends. And how to still have faith while facing pain and suffering in the face. I'm never going to stop asking questions and thinking, but whether it's a struggle of sin relationships in the church, or in my family, or whether it be the intellectual questions I can't answer, I'm not going to choose either of the immoral options—of either settling for the simplistic answers that close down the mind and take away the pain, or of aligning myself with the modern, intellectual smart-aleck who simply leaves lesser mortals with no answers, no hope, no direction, no rationality and no sanity in the final analysis.

I want to say with conviction, not believing that I abdicate from using what intelligence God has given me, not escaping the sheer hard work of intellectual study or reading, that the words of Jesus to John the Baptist are a wonderful focal point that will help you live with all your loose ends without taking the insecure option of needing constantly to have 'certain' answers. Jesus said, 'How happy are those who have no doubts about me!' (GNB).

There is a poster which says 'He is the still point of a

turning world.' You will learn to live with the loose ends, you will even come to love the untidiness of mind, of not being able to answer all the questions, if you allow Jesus to be the one stabilising still point of your turning world. His life, his teaching, his consistency, his passion, his courage, his self-giving have inspired the lives and minds of countless humanitarians and intellectuals from Tolstoi to Mother Teresa; Bonnhoeffer to St Francis of Assisi. This experiential, well-attested fact, has been magnificently evidenced in the lives of generation after generation of human beings over the last two thousand years.

Jesus named John the Baptist as the best, hottest, godliest preacher the world had ever seen. John sat in a prison full of doubts about the central point of his own message—Jesus. He was in theological crisis about Jesus and that was the only thing he'd ever lived for, to preach the coming of the Messiah. His identity, his being, his self-worth were shattered in that prison and he was about to die. And Jesus gave no answers as to why.

And in the midst of all that, petty little Jerusalem theological nuisances came with their seminary irrelevancy, so to speak, and argued about the appropriateness, for the image of good and godly morality, for Jesus to be hanging out at Matthew's parties of outcasts. They said 'How come?' Jesus replied, 'John the Baptist didn't drink. He did it exactly as you want of me. It was neat and clean. The ends were tied up. He lived out in the desert. He didn't get compromised by naughty people, and came out and preached the Kingdom. And you said he was a fanatic because he didn't integrate into the society. I come, the Son of Man comes eating and drinking, and you say "Look at him, he's a glutton and a wine bibber!" '

Loose ends—conflicts! contradictions! complications! In the midst of which Jesus says 'How happy are those who have no doubts about me.'

My dear friends, you can live with multitudes of loose ends if Jesus is the still point of your turning world—and you live on the cutting edge with him.

ACKNOWLEDGEMENTS

Many people have helped in the preparation of this book. I should particularly like to thank:

Elizabeth Gibson, who edited the transcribed material into shape.

Pat Cruse, who transcribed more than 190,000 words from tape at the outset of the book's preparation.

Martin Wroe, who had the original idea.

Trevor Chambers, my researcher, for his assistance with research, editing, proof-reading and helping to put together the final text.

Steve Drury, my manager, who helped with organisation and professional negotiation to see this book through to publication.

Alan Harvey who helped with editing and proof-reading.

Andrea Charles who assisted in both typing and proof-reading.

To one and all, my grateful thanks.

If you would like to write to John Smith or his organisation, please use the following address:

> Care and Communication Concern,
> PO Box 463,
> Boronia 3155,
> Victoria,
> AUSTRALIA